DR. DAEMON JONES

author of *Daelicious! Recipes for Vibrant Living*

Where science, flavor and health meet deliciousness!

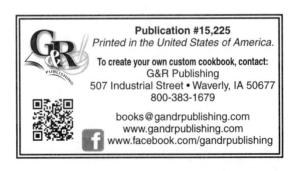

Publication #15,225
Printed in the United States of America.

To create your own custom cookbook, contact:
G&R Publishing
507 Industrial Street • Waverly, IA 50677
800-383-1679

books@gandrpublishing.com
www.gandrpublishing.com
www.facebook.com/gandrpublishing

Acknowledgements

It has been a wonderful, but scary process for me to share my passion and my beliefs with the world. My mission is to create better health through using food as a delicious form of medicine. I found myself in a very vulnerable place by asking people to abandon their norm to try something different. I would not have had the courage to create this book or go to through the publishing process without the love and support of my family and close friends. So I would like to take a moment to give special acknowledgements to:

• My mother and brother, Daryl for being a sounding board for my ideas and giving me the thumbs up to step out a little farther than I thought I could.

• Wendy Wormal, my accountability partner, who never lets me give up on my goals. Wendy you have helped me stay focused on getting this done. You never let me step too far away from the plan. Thank you for the gentle reminders to keep sharing my insights to help create a healthier world. It is worth it!

• My angel on earth Gina Green, who is the greatest friend on the planet!

• My foodies: Jennifer Benn, Lisa Copeland, Daryl Jones, DeBorah Posey, Valerie Samuell and Theresa Stone. Thank you for trying my recipes and helping me to get them from good to great!

• William Grant, VI, my brother from another mother, who created the front and back covers. Your artwork is perfect. I'm so excited we are working on project together. I'm sure this is the first of many more to come!

• And special thanks to my editor, Tiffany Snyder, who stepped into this project at a time of crisis and pulled all the pieces together. Your commitment to this project and your belief that this book had something to offer the world was priceless. Thank you for making a difficult situation seem easy. Thank you for putting me back on track to get this complete and ready for the world.

Table of Contents

Introduction IV

Food Information
    A Plant-Based Diet VI
    Serving Sizes for Proteins............................... IX
    Eating Seasonally XI
    The Whole Foods Pantry XIII
    Eating Healthy Economically XV
    Sample Menus... XVII

Recipes
    Great Beginnings..1
    Satisfying Soups 21
    Spectacularly Simple Salads.......................... 33
    Exciting Entrees 57
    Whole Grains Goodness................................ 79
    Vibrant Vegetables 91
    Supercharged Snacks................................. 111
    Daelicious Desserts 123

Bibliography..A

About the Author

Index...i

Introduction

I want people to understand that cooking and eating healthy food can and should be a delicious and fun activity to be shared with loved ones, family, friends, and their communities. Food is beautiful, and should be considered a joy for the eyes, nose, taste buds and tummy. I want you and all Americans to be more connected with your food. I want you to understand the benefit of whole foods. I want you to become more conscious about what you are putting into your mouth. I want you to understand that eating well gives you energy and the ability to achieve all of your life goals and dreams. Eating poorly robs you of your energy, your vitality, the health of your cells, and eventually the health of your body--which is something you may not be aware of.

More and more research is finding this simple truth--plant-based foods reverse and prevent disease. Here is one fantastic example, the EPIC (The European Prospective Investigation into Cancer and Nutrition) study followed more than half a million (521, 000) participants recruited across 10 European countries for almost 15 years. It is the largest study looking at the relationship between lifestyle and cancer risk. It found that chronic diseases can be prevented and reversed by eating a plant-based diet. The more plant-based foods we have on our plate, the healthier we feel, the younger we look, and the better our quality of life.

I decided to focus on anti-aging, diabetes, heart disease and obesity because I deal with them most frequently in my practice. While they all have different symptoms and affect people in different ways, they all have a common underlying cause--chronic inflammation. Chronic inflammation damages and destroys cells, uses up vitamins and nutrients the body needs, and depletes our energy and energy reserves. This puts our organs at risk for early cell death (pre mature aging) or dysfunction (heart disease, diabetes, obesity). Nature's correction to chronic or long term inflammation is found in vitamins, minerals and nutrients that are abundant in plant-based foods – fruit, vegetables, nuts, seeds, grains, beans and legumes.

The purpose of this book is to introduce the concept of simple, delicious plant-based foods that support your body's ability to be at its best. Many people believe there are virtues to becoming vegetarian, but they don't think they can do it because they believe the meals will not be tasty or satisfying.

Neither of these beliefs are true. This is a great starter book for those who want to explore a plant-based diet, but are not sure how to do it. If you are a seasoned vegan, this book will give you some new twists on old favorites and teach you more about how your food is serving your health.

The greatest gift you can give yourself is to use delicious foods as the foundation for your best health! This book has been created to support you in achieving your health goals in a delicious way. Thank you for supporting my efforts to create a healthier, whole foods, plant-based world.

Daemon Jones, ND

Eat More Plants!

Where science, flavor and health meet deliciousness

A Plant-Based Diet

A plant-based diet starts with whole foods. The concept of whole foods simply refers to eating foods in their natural state. Foods are categorized in three types: proteins, carbohydrates and fats. Whole foods are defined as foods coming from or living on the earth at one time. These foods have a high nutrient density, essential and non-essential amino acids, essential fatty acids, phytochemicals, fiber, and micronutrients required for metabolism and restoration.

Proteins

Plant–based proteins are a requirement for daily nutrition. Some excellent protein dense plant-based nutrition choices are nuts, seeds, beans, legumes and some whole grains. Almonds, pecans, walnuts and cashews are great examples of nut proteins. Protein from legumes can be found in pinto beans, navy beans, green peas, string beans, lentils, black-eyed peas, chickpeas (garbanzo beans), lima beans and soy beans (tofu).

Carbohydrates

The carbohydrate category is composed of grains, vegetables and fruits. Whole grains include any grain that has the fiber part of the grain still intact. Examples are steel cut oats, millet, barley, brown rice, wild rice, amaranth, quinoa, couscous, spelt, bran and corn.

When choosing bread, cereal and pasta, beware of labels that read "wheat flour", "unbleached wheat flour" or "enriched wheat flour". They are not acceptable, so be careful. Look for the words "whole grain". Grains are an important part of this category, however it is important to eat more servings of fruits and veggies than grains on a daily basis.

Although vegetables and fruits are carbohydrates, they're also healthy sources of fiber, micronutrients and phytonutrients. When choosing fruits and vegetables, try to incorporate as many colors of the rainbow as possible each day. Select yellow, orange, blue, green, red, purple and white fruits and vegetables to ensure that you are consuming a variety of nutrients. Perhaps you like local fruits and vegetables or maybe you prefer exotic varieties from other countries. Experiment with different types and varieties and you will find a plethora of options that are delicious and satisfying.

I always recommend that you eat seasonally when fruits and vegetables are the freshest and have the most flavor.

There are several different ways to eat and enjoy vegetables. Eat as many raw, sautéed, roasted, blanched or pureed vegetables as possible. I recommend up to 10 servings per day.

Fruits are a wonderful source of flavonoids, carotenoids and antioxidants. The more colorful the fruit, the more nutrients are available for your body. Fresh fruits are always best. Small amounts of dried fruit are also acceptable, although they do contain more sugar. Fruits are wonderful to sprinkle in the diet. I recommend at least 2 servings per day. Limit dried fruits to no more than one serving per day because they become sweeter and add more sugar to the diet when dried. They are best in small servings, as part of a meal.

Fats

The best oils are found in nuts, seeds, avocados and coconut. Olive, walnut and sesame oils are good for cooking at lower temperatures. Coconut, safflower, sunflower and peanut oils have a high boiling temperature. Others, like flaxseed oil are good for salad dressing but not for cooking because the boiling point is low.

Avoid hydrogenated oils and trans-fatty acids as they have been implicated in disease-forming processes in the body. Hydrogenated or partially hydrogenated oils are hidden in margarine, vegetable shortening, non-dairy whipped dessert toppings, cake and cake frosting, Asian crunchy noodles, crackers, frozen dinners, white bread, non-dairy coffee creamers, tortillas, fast food, donuts, peanut butter, ice cream, cookies, microwave popcorn, French fries, pie crusts, pancakes, waffles and anything fried.

A vegan plant-based diet includes no animal products. The phytonutrients and fiber found in a plant-based diet support the lymphatic system, as well as the immune system's ability to increase health outcomes. The reduction of saturated fats from animal products supports the body's restorative and healing process. This is especially important in anti-aging as well as heart disease, diabetes or other chronic, energy-depleting health conditions.

It is important with a plant-based diet to include sources of protein with each meal and in each day's intake. Plant-based proteins are generally derived from nuts, seeds, legumes and beans. However, proteins are also found in low amounts in most whole grains and vegetables.

The key to having balanced meals while eating a plant-based diet is to make sure you have a combination of proteins, carbohydrates and healthy fats. Here are serving sizes for each.

Fruits and vegetables are roughly ½ cup cooked or 1 cup of raw.

Whole Grains are generally ½ cup cooked, 1 ounce uncooked or 1 slice of bread.

A serving size of protein is as stated below.

Meats Alternative and Legumes:

Tofu	½ cup/ 4 ounces	10g
Firm Tofu	½ cup/ 4 ounces	20g
Tempeh	½ cup/ 3 ounces	16g
Seitan	¼ cup/ 2 ounces	14g
Textured soy protein	½ cup/ 4 ounces	11g

Grains:

Amaranth	½ cup	14g
Barley	½ cup	10g
Buckwheat	½ cup	3g
Millet	½ cup	4g
Dark rye flour	½ cup	9g
Oats	½ cup	3g
Quinoa	½ cup	11g
Brown rice	½ cup	3g
White rice	½ cup	3g
Soy flour (low-fat)	½ cup	20g

Non-Dairy substitutes:

Soy milk	1 cup	6g
Rice milk	1 cup	1g
Almond	1 cup	3-4g

Nuts/Seeds:

Nuts . . . . ¼ cup 8g
Seeds . . . . 2 tablespoon. 3g
Nut butter . . . . 2 tablespoon. 8g
Seed butter. . . . . 2 tablespoon. 5g

Whole beans:

Whole beans. . . . . ½ cup. 7g
Lentils . . . . ½ cup. 9g
Refried beans . . . . ½ cup. 8g
Garden burger . . . . 1 . . . . .11g
Soy Burger . . . . 1 . . . . .11g

Miscellaneous:

Vegetables . . . . ½ cup. 1-2g
Fruit. 1 0
Bread . . . . 1 slice. 1-5g
Flour tortilla. . . . . 1 . . . . .3g
Miso . . . . 2 tablespoon. 4g
Soy cheese . . . . 1 ounce 4-7g
Soy yogurt . . . . 1 cup 6g
Non-dairy creamer . . . . . 1 cup 1g
Protein powder . . . . 1 tablespoon. 9-15g
                              1 ounce 26g
Spirulina . . . . 1 teaspoon 8g
                              1 ounce 16g
Brewer's yeast. . . . . 1 tablespoon. 3g
                              1 ounce 11g

Note: If you're choosing a totally plant-based or vegan lifestyle, you have to make sure that you're taking a good B12 supplement. Plant-based food sources do not have significant amounts of B12 and could cause a B12 deficiency over time. Supplementing with high quality B12 oral supplements, B12 intramuscular shots or intravenous (IV) B12 will prevent the deficiency. Consult with your physician to check your B12 levels and to get advice on best way to supplement.

Eat Seasonally

One of the gifts of eating a plant-based diet is enjoying seasonal foods. When fruits and vegetables are at the peak of ripeness they are bursting with flavors and nutrients at the same time.

Have you ever had a craving for a nice ripe slice of watermelon or a fresh juicy peach in the heat of summer? When there is snow on the ground, have you yearned for a hearty bowl of chili or a stew filled with chunks of vegetables? These cravings indicate our bodies' longing for seasonal foods. When we listen to our bodies, we are listening to nature's way of bringing us into greater harmony through healing foods.

Eating seasonally can be an important part of your health plan. When you are eating seasonally, your diet is rich in nutrient dense whole foods. Choose locally grown foods because they will be the freshest options from farm to table. When you eat seasonally, you will be eating food that will have your taste buds jumping for joy.

Here is a starter list of foods to consider incorporating in your diet each season:

Spring

Spring is the time of new beginnings and renewals. Vegetables are springing up all over the place. Strawberries and spinach are two of my favorites. Other spring vegetables are asparagus, artichokes, chards, broccoli, collard greens, fava beans, fennel, green beans, mustard greens, peas, pea pods, snow peas, rhubarb and Vidalia onions. Lettuces are abundant too, here are some examples: Belgian endive, butter lettuce, Manoa lettuce, red leaf lettuce, spring baby lettuce and radicchio. Herbs are a fantastic way to incorporate additional nutrients to your meals. Chives, mint and scallions are great choices to add flavor.

Summer

Summer is filled with long days and more opportunities to play and vacation. Warmer weather and increased outdoor activity brings about the need to feel cooler and lighter. Summer is a time of fruit, fruit and more fruit! Our bodies

X

crave foods that are full of water. Apricots, peaches, plums, grapes, cantaloupes, cherries, figs, grapefruits, melons, limes, lychee, nectarines, passion fruits and watermelon are aplenty. If berries are your thing, blueberries, blackberries, raspberries, boysenberries, black currants and mulberries are coming into fruition.

Vegetables like beets, bell peppers, Chinese long beans, cucumbers, eggplant, garlic, edamame, jalapeno peppers, lima beans, okra, peas, radishes, shallots, sugar snap peas, summer squash, tomatillo, tomatoes, Yukon gold potatoes and zucchini are in season and readily available in summer.

Autumn

Autumn is harvest time, so there is a bounty of choices. The days begin to shorten and the temperature begins to drop in the evenings. Autumn is the time for building and preparing for winter. We are building up our systems with more hearty foods than we did in the summer. We crave comfort foods that contain more grains, vegetables and proteins, including nuts and seeds. Fall fruits like pears, apples, quinces, persimmons and grapes are plentiful and ready to be used in all or our recipes.

Root vegetables like beets, carrots, potatoes and yams are good too. Squashes come in so many different types -- acorn, butternut, spaghetti, pumpkin, chayote, delicata and zucchini, just to name a few. Grains are great to add to your meals. Proteins, especially beans, nuts and seeds make a meal hearty and filling.

Winter

The days are even shorter and it is getting colder. We think about staying indoors and we want heavier warming foods. Look forward to vegetables like Brussel sprouts, butternut squash, collard greens, delicata squash, kale, leeks, sweet potatoes, turnips, winter squash, carrots, onions, garlic and potatoes. There are a few fruits to enjoy in the winter months like clementine, dates, kiwi, oranges, pear, persimmons, pomegranates and tangerines.

If you plan to eat seasonally, you will be eating a whole food diet.

The Whole Foods Pantry

Once you have made the commitment to change your eating habits to include more plant-based foods, the next step is preparation. Having a well-stocked pantry makes cooking a quicker and more pleasurable experience. This list primarily includes non-perishable items that are used frequently when making anything from breakfast to stews. Once you get in the swing of cooking and discovering new recipes, you will see which items you use most.

To make stocking your pantry cost-effective, I suggest that you choose a couple of recipes you like and buy those ingredients. Then, once a week or once a month, buy another staple or two. Over time, you will have a well-stocked pantry. Many communities have health food stores with bulk sections. This is a great way to buy herbs, grains, legumes and dried fruit in larger quantities at a cheaper price than your local grocery store. You might have to make a special trip once a month, but for the savings, it will be worth it.

Herbs & Spices – Fresh and/or Dry

Allspice	Ginger
Basil	Italian seasoning
Bay leaves	Mint
Black pepper	Dried mustard
Cayenne pepper	Nutmeg
Chives	Oregano
Cinnamon	Parsley
Coriander	Rosemary
Cumin	Sage
Curry	Sea salt
Dill	Thyme
Garlic	Vanilla extract

Nuts

Almonds	Pine nuts
Cashews	Walnuts
Pecans	

Grains and Dried Foods

Baking soda
Baking powder
Couscous
Dried cranberries
Dried mushrooms

Lentils, green and pink
Oats
Gluten free flour

Popcorn
Quinoa
Raisins
Raw sugar (turbinado)
Rice – brown, wild rice,
    long grain
Whole wheat flour
Whole wheat noodles
Gluten free noodles

Oil and Condiments

Apple cider vinegar
Balsamic vinegar

Extra virgin olive oil
Ghee
Maple Syrup
Nut butters – Peanut butter
Almond butter
Vegetable broth – organic
White wine vinegar

Red wine vinegar
Rice milk, soy milk,
    almond milk,
oat milk
Rice wine vinegar
Safflower or sunflower oil
Sesame oil
Soy sauce or tamari
(wheat-free soy sauce)

Perishables

Carrots
Garlic
Hot peppers
Limes/lemons
Mushrooms
Onions

Salad greens
Scallions
Seasonal fruit/vegetables
Sweet potatoes
Tomatoes – fresh
Whole Wheat tortillas

Canned Goods

Tomato sauce
Tomato paste
Olives

Stewed tomatoes
Canned beans – chickpeas,
    black beans, white beans

Frozen foods

Mixed vegetables
Corn
Seasonal Fruits – berries,
bananas, peaches, pineapples

Spinach
Whole grain bread/Gluten
Free breads

Healthy Options: Eating Whole Foods Economically

When I first suggest to patients that they should consider a healthy plant-based diet, I often hear, "I can't afford to eat healthy–it's too expensive". I disagree. You can always start to make better food choices without breaking the bank.

The first step in changing to a plant-based diet is to change your perception of what is healthy. You can buy healthy options, even if they are not organic. Choose healthy whole foods instead of processed, prepackaged, or refined foods. Whole foods like beans, nuts, seeds, vegetables, fruits and whole grains can usually be found around the perimeter of the grocery store. Cookies, cakes, frozen pizza, pasta, sugary cereals and the like are not examples of whole foods. They are usually found in the interior of the store.

Let me give you a financial example. A box of high sugar cereal costs much more than a box of oatmeal (not individually sized packets). Make the healthy and economical choice. Watch for weekly specials on produce, and use your pantry list to choose staples when they are on sale. Health food stores and some larger grocery chains sell grains, cereals, dried beans, nuts, seeds, herbs, and dried fruits in bulk. This is a great way to buy items in the quantities that you need and for a price that can fit into your budget. If you have the option to shop at ethnic markets, like Asian or Hispanic markets, you can often find fresh produce for less than the larger groceries stores' prices.

Whenever possible, I recommend that you use foods that are pesticide and hormone free-- in other words, organic. Eating organic foods reduces the toxic load on the body. If you can't buy everything organic, try to avoid the 'dirty dozen'. The 'dirty dozen' is the Environmental Working Group's list of the top twelve conventionally grown fruits and vegetables most heavily laden with pesticides: peaches, apples, sweet bell peppers, celery, nectarines, strawberries, cherries, lettuce, imported grapes, pears, spinach and potatoes. Buy these organic whenever you can. (For the complete list, see (www.ewg.org)

Also consider finding your local farmers' market. Ask the farmers if they use pesticides. Some smaller farms do not use pesticides but can't call their produce 'organic' because of legal definitions and costs involved. This is a good healthy option where we can save money as well. Also, look for half-price bins of slightly bruised produce at health food stores or farmers' markets. You can cut the bruised part off and salvage the rest for your recipes.

One of my favorite cost-effective tricks is to buy seeds or little herb plants from a nursery or farmers' market and grow them to use in the kitchen. You can spend $10. for 4 or 5 plants and use them all year long. Place them in a sunny windowsill, water them regularly, and when you're ready to cook, pinch off what you need. If you have children this is a wonderful teaching tool, and it gets children excited about trying foods that they have watched grow.

Sample Menus: Ideas to create a Balanced Meal

One of the questions people ask me all the time is how I put recipes together to create a delicious meal. Here are some sample ideas of how to make a great meal.

You can come up with your own our choices and share them with me on Facebook at www.facebook.com/HealthyDaes or twitter, @DrDae.

Comforting Carrot Soup
Tofu Scramble
Basic Brussels Sprouts

Black Bean Salsa with Guacamole
Minty Summer Squash
Quinoa
Tuck into pita bread or rolled into a tortilla

Simple Barley
Sweet Sautéed Kale
Fruit-Filled Acorn Squash

Fantastically Fresh Tomato Soup
Whole Wheat Pasta Medley
Poached Pears

Bok Choy Stir Fry
Simply Barley
Marinated Kale & Carrot Salad

Lime Coconut Chickpeas
Simply Barley
Sweet Potato Pie

Bok Choy Stir Fry
Orange Rosemary Salad
Nutty Rice with Mushrooms

Nut Loaf
Mushroom Gravy
Curried Chard
Butternut Squash with Quinoa

Vegetarian Lettuce Wraps
Butternut Squash and Quinoa
Kabocha Squash Pie

Great Beginnings

Banana Bliss Pancakes

Everyone loves pancakes! This recipe has a balance of soluble fiber, healthy oils and protein that ward off sugar spikes and crashes. Balanced blood sugar levels prevent the storage of extra sugar as body fat. This is a gluten-free option as long as you use gluten-free oats. Makes 4 servings.

2 bananas

2 teaspoons of ground flax seeds

2 teaspoons of coconut oil

1/2 teaspoon of vanilla extract

1/4 cup of almond milk (or other substitute)

2 teaspoons of maple syrup

1 cup of gluten-free oat flour*

1 teaspoon baking powder

1/2 teaspoon of cinnamon

1 pinch nutmeg

Coconut oil for cooking

Garnish

1/2 cup of walnuts

1 banana cut into slices

1. In a large bowl place the bananas and mash them up into a pudding like consistency. Add flax seeds, coconut oil, vanilla, almond milk and maple syrup; mix well.
2. *In a blender or a grinder take the gluten-free oats and grind until they become meal or flour.
3. In a small bowl add the oat flour, baking powder, cinnamon and nutmeg; mix together, then add to the wet ingredients in the large bowl.
4. Let the batter rest for 5 minutes.
5. Add a teaspoon of coconut oil to a cast iron skillet.
6. Add about 2 tablespoons of the batter; cook for about 3 minutes on each side. (Both sides should be brown and slightly crunchy).
7. Serve with walnuts, fresh banana slices and a touch of maple syrup.

Prep time: 10 minutes
Cook time: 15 minutes

Nutrients per serving: Calories: 399, Total Fat: 15 g, Sat. Fat: 2 g, Carbs: 56 g, Fiber: 7 g, Sugars: 10 g, Protein: 13 g, Sodium: 18 mg, Cholesterol: 0 mg

Chia Seed Raspberry Jam

This jam is lovely on toast or used as a healthy alternative in your kids' peanut butter and jelly sandwiches. You can use grapes or strawberries as a substitute for the raspberries. Chia seeds are a great source of Omega 3 fatty acids. Omega 3 fatty acids have strong anti-inflammatory and anti-aging properties that are important for tissue repair and rejuvenation of cells. Chia seeds become gelatinous in liquids, so the combination makes a great jam or jelly. Makes 8 servings.

1 cup of raspberries

1 tablespoon of chia seed, ground

1 tablespoon of warm water

1 tablespoon of maple syrup

1. Place all the ingredients in a blender.
2. Mix for 1 minute.
3. Chill for 1 hour before serving.

Prep time: 5 minutes

Nutrients per serving: Calories: 32, Total Fat: 1 g, Sat. Fat: 0 g, Carbs: 5 g, Fiber: 2 g, Sugars: 2 g, Protein: 1 g, Sodium: 1 mg, Cholesterol: 0 mg

"Don't eat anything your great-grandmother wouldn't recognize as food."
~ Michael Pollan

Old Fashioned Oatmeal

This is a classic warm breakfast treat. Steel cut oats have more fiber and make a heartier meal than quick oatmeal flakes. One of oatmeal's health benefits is found in its soluble fiber. Soluble fiber binds to cholesterol and cholesterol based hormones and pulls them into the digestive tract so they can be eliminated from the body. Anyone with cholesterol issues should make oatmeal a part of their diet. You can use the leftovers in the oatmeal smoothie. Makes 8 servings.

2 cups of water

1 cup of steel cut oats

1/4 cup of dried cranberries

2 tablespoons of maple syrup

1/2 teaspoon of ground cinnamon

1/4 teaspoon of ginger, ground

1/4 - 1/2 cup of rice milk or milk substitute

1/4 cup of walnuts

1. In a 4 quart pot, bring water to a boil.
2. Add steel cut oats, dried cranberries, maple syrup, cinnamon, and ginger.
3. Cover and cook at a simmer for 20 minutes or until water has been absorbed.
4. Remove from heat and add rice milk and walnuts.

Prep time: 5 minutes
Cook time: 20 minutes

Nutrients per serving: Calories: 142, Total Fat: 4 g, Sat. Fat: 0 g, Carbs: 24 g, Fiber: 3 g, Sugars: 8 g, Protein: 4 g, Sodium: 7 mg, Cholesterol: 0 mg

"True healthcare reform starts in your kitchen, not in Washington"
~Anonymous

Quick Quinoa Breakfast

Did you know that quinoa is actually a seed, but it is often used in place of grains? Quinoa makes for a breakfast that warms your heart, fuels your brain and keeps you satiated. The protein from quinoa and almonds make this breakfast heartier than it seems by adding protein. The fiber from the pear fill you up, keeping you satiated while lowering cholesterol and improving heart health. Makes 6 servings.

1 1/2 cup of rice milk or other milk substitute

1/2 teaspoon of ground cardamom

1/2 teaspoon of ginger, grated

1 cup of quinoa, rinsed

1 pear sliced

1/4 cup of raisins or dried blueberries

1/2 cup of sliced almonds

1 teaspoon of maple syrup

1. In a saucepan, add rice milk, cardamom and ginger; bring to a slow boil.
2. Rinse quinoa 3-4 times through a sieve.
3. Add quinoa and cook for 15 minutes or until milk is absorbed.
4. Remove from heat.
5. Add pear, raisins, almonds and maple syrup. Enjoy!

Prep time: 5 minutes
Cook time: 15 minutes

Nutrients per serving: Calories: 385, Total Fat: 9 g, Sat. Fat: 1 g, Carbs: 54 g, Fiber: 6 g, Sugars: 11 g, Protein: 9 g, Sodium: 36 mg, Cholesterol: 0 mg

"Just because you're not sick doesn't mean you're healthy"
~Author Unknown

Sautéed Apples

In my family, we always called these "fried apples" and they would be served with breakfast as a sweet treat. Apples have a phytonutrient called quercitin which prevents damage to cell walls and the DNA inside the cell. This is probably where apples earned their reputation: an apple a day keeps the doctor away. Adding some toasted walnuts makes this even better. The walnuts' omega-3 essential acids reduce inflammation in the body. Inflammation is common in heart disease, high cholesterol, diabetes, and any disease that causes you pain every day. Make 4 servings.

1/2 cup of walnuts

4 Granny Smith apples, sliced into wedges

1/4 cup of turbinado sugar

1/2 teaspoon of cinnamon

1/2 teaspoon of lemon juice

Zest of one lemon

2 teaspoons of coconut oil

1. Pre-heat the oven to 375 °F.
2. On a cooking sheet, add parchment paper; spread out the walnuts.
3. Bake for 5-7 minutes.
4. In a bowl, add apples, sugar, cinnamon, 1/2 of the lemon juice and lemon zest; combine well.
5. Heat coconut oil over medium; add mixture.
6. Cook for 7-10 minutes, then sprinkle remaining lemon juice over top.
7. Sprinkle walnuts over top of the apples.

You can make a double batch and blend the leftovers to make applesauce.

Prep time: 5 minutes
Cook time: 17 minutes

Nutrients per serving: Calories: 202, Total Fat: 11 g, Sat. Fat: 2 g, Carbs: 27 g, Fiber: 6 g, Sugars: 19 g, Protein: 4 g, Sodium: 2 mg, Cholesterol: 0 mg

Sweet Potato Hash Browns

*I love to have hash browns with my breakfast.
They are a crunchy treat. For a change, I used sweet potatoes
for extra fiber and nutrients instead of traditional potatoes.
The sweet potatoes and apples are great a combination
of soluble fiber that is tasty and great for your heart and
balancing blood sugars. Make 6 servings.*

2 tablespoons of chia seeds ground

6 tablespoons of water

4 medium sized sweet potatoes, grated

1 medium sized-apple, grated

1/2 teaspoon of sea salt

3 tablespoons of flour (wheat or gluten-free flour)

1 teaspoon of cinnamon

2 teaspoons of Coconut oil

1. In a small bowl, combine chia seeds and water.
2. Refrigerate for 10-15 minutes. If you can refrigerate for up to 1 hour you will have more gelatinous consistency.
3. In a large colander, combine sweet potatoes and apples and drain any extra water.
4. Add sweet potatoes and apples to a large bowl.
5. Combine sea salt, chia seeds, flour and cinnamon in the large bowl. Mix until combined.
6. In a saucepan, add oil and sauté for 2 minutes on each side.
7. Remove from oil and place on a plate with a paper towel to remove excess oil.
8. Serve with applesauce.

Prep time: 5 minutes
Cook time: 17 minutes

Nutrients per serving: Calories: 176, Total Fat: 2 g, Sat. Fat: 0 g, Carbs: 36 g, Fiber: 8 g, Sugars: 11 g, Protein: 4 g, Sodium: 227 mg, Cholesterol: 0 mg

"The human animal is adapted to, and apparently can thrive on, an extraordinary range of different diets, but the Western diet, however you define it, does not seem to be one of them."
~ Michael Pollan, In defense of Food: An Eater's manifesto

Tofu Scramble

The secret to cooking with tofu is to remove it from the package and place a weighted object on top of it to remove excess water. Removing the water allows the tofu to take on the flavor of whatever it is cooked in. Make 6 servings.

1 pound of firm tofu
4 garlic cloves, minced
1 cup of yellow onion, chopped
1 cup of bell peppers, chopped (red, orange and green)

2 teaspoons of extra virgin olive oil
1/2 teaspoon of turmeric
1 teaspoon of fresh parsley, chopped
Sea salt and pepper to taste

1. Remove tofu from the package, place on a paper towel with a plate on top and let drain for a few minutes.
2. Sauté garlic, onion, peppers and oil in a sauté pan for 4 minutes.
3. Crumble the tofu into the pan. Add the spices and cook for another 5 minutes. Serve immediately.

Prep time: 10 minutes
Cook time: 10 minutes

Nut Nutrients per serving: Calories: 79, Total Fat: 4 g, Sat. Fat: 1 g, Carbs: 6 g, Fiber: 1 g, Sugars: 3 g, Protein: 6 g, Sodium: 30 mg, Cholesterol: 0 mg

"Eat food. Not too much. Mostly plants."
~ Michael Pollan, In Defense of Food: An Eater's Manifesto

Pumpkin Bread

My 4 year-old nephew loves to make this recipe with his mom and you will too. The pumpkin and whole wheat flour introduce fiber while still adding a little sweetness to your morning. I love to toast a slice and spread a tablespoon of nut butter on top. Pumpkins are high in beta carotene and Vitamin A which are crucial nutrients for healing wounds and repairing cells. Makes 8 servings.

2 tablespoons of ground flaxseeds with 6 tablespoons of water (to use as a egg substitute)

6 tablespoons of vegan butter substitute (or applesauce)

2/3 cups of turbinado sugar

1 cup of mashed pumpkin

1 teaspoon of vanilla extract

3/4 cup of whole wheat flour

3/4 cup of unbleached flour

1 teaspoon of baking soda

1 teaspoon of ground ginger

1/2 teaspoon of ground nutmeg

1/2 teaspoon of ground allspice

1/4 teaspoon of baking powder

1/3-1/2 cup of your favorite milk substitute

1. Preheat oven to 350°F.
2. Use 1 tablespoon of ground flaxseeds with 3 tablespoons water. Stir together until thick and gelatinous.
3 In a large bowl add the vegan butter substitute, turbinado sugar, pumpkin and vanilla. Mix for 1 minutes.
4. In another bowl, mix the dry ingredients: whole wheat flour, unbleached flour, baking soda, ground ginger, ground nutmeg, ground allspice and baking powder.
5. Slowly stir the dry ingredients into the wet ingredients. Once all of the ingredients have been combined, add the milk substitute.
6. Pour the batter into the loaf pan and bake for 55-65 minutes or until a toothpick stuck in the middle comes out clean.

Prep time: 5 minutes
Bake time: 55-65 minutes

Nutrients per serving: Calories: 260, Total Fat: 11 g, Sat. Fat: 5 g, Carbs: 38 g, Fiber: 2 g, Sugars: 7 g, Protein: 3 g, Sodium: 161 mg, Cholesterol: 0 mg

Avocado Delight

By far, this smoothie is a fan favorite. You will be amazed by how fruity and delicious this recipe tastes. Avocado is a great source of essential fatty acids and fiber which makes it a super food. It helps with diabetes and promotes heart health. The anti-inflammatory properties make it a star for anti-aging. Makes 2 servings of 12 ounces each.

1/4 cup of fresh mashed avocado

1/2 cup of rice milk or other milk substitute

1 teaspoon of agave nectar

1/2 frozen banana

1/2 cup of frozen mango pieces

1/4 cup of frozen peaches

1/4 cup of apple juice

1. In a blender, add avocado, milk. agave, banana, mango, peach pieces, apple juice and whip 60 seconds or until smooth.
2. Freeze leftover smoothie. (To reuse, defrost for about 10 minutes, then place in blender for 40 seconds.)

Prep time: 5 minutes

Nutrients per serving: Calories: 139, Total Fat: 4 g, Sat. Fat: 0 g, Carbs: 28 g, Fiber: 3 g, Sugars: 16 g, Protein: 1 g, Sodium: 23 mg, Cholesterol: 0 mg

Almond Coconut Smoothie

Almonds have monounsaturated fats which are the healthy fats that help lower the bad cholesterol and the risk of heart disease. The medium-chain saturated fatty acids in coconut milk help with digestion and may also help with improving overall blood lipids levels like cholesterol or triglycerides. The coconut milk is the liquid base. It adds a smoothness and nice texture to your smoothie. Makes 2 servings of 12 ounces each.

1/2 cup of coconut milk

1 cup of water

1/2 cup of almonds

1/2 -1 teaspoon of almond extract

1 teaspoon of agave nectar

Add all ingredients to a blender and combine until smooth, about 1 minute.

Prep time: 5 minutes

Nutrients per serving: Calories: 326, Total Fat: 30 g, Sat. Fat: 12 g, Carbs: 11 g, Fiber: 4 g, Sugars: 3 g, Protein: 9 g, Sodium: 9 mg, Cholesterol: 0 mg

Oatmeal Smoothie

*Horchata is a Costa Rican smoothie made with oatmeal
and it is such a treat. I made a version of Horchata filled with
fiber to support heart health and to balance blood sugar.
This smoothie is perfect after any workout.
Makes 2 servings of 8 ounces each.*

1/2 cup of oatmeal, cooked

1 cup of almond milk or milk
  substitute

1/2 banana, peeled

1-2 teaspoons of black strap
  molasses

1/2 teaspoon of vanilla
  extract

1/4-1/2 teaspoon of
  cinnamon

Add all ingredients to a blender and combine until smooth,
about 1 minute.

Prep time: 5 minutes

Nutrients per serving: Calories: 289, Total Fat: 2 g, Sat. Fat: 0
g, Carbs: 37 g, Fiber: 3 g, Sugars: 13 g, Protein: 2 g, Sodium:
74 mg, Cholesterol: 1 mg

Chocolate Peanut Butter Cup Smoothie

*I just can't help myself. I love combining chocolate and peanut
butter because it is soooo good. When we think about health
benefits of peanuts usually we think protein, but peanuts
are high in antioxidants too. Combining peanuts with dark
chocolate makes this smoothie an anti-aging, anti-cancer,
anti-inflammatory powerhouse. The fiber, magnesium and
Vitamin E are nutrient bonuses. Since cocoa is not sweet by
nature you might find that you need to add a little sweetness to
smooth out the taste. Makes 2 servings of 8 ounces each.*

1/4 cup of peanut butter

1 tablespoon of dark cocoa
  powder or use a chocolate
  protein powder

1/2 of a frozen banana

1 cup of soy milk (or milk
  alternative)

*1 teaspoon of raw turbinado
  sugar, to taste

In a blender add all ingredients and blend for 1 minute.

Prep time: 5 minutes

Nutrients per serving: Calories: 289, Total Fat: 19 g, Sat. Fat: 4
g, Carbs: 23 g, Fiber: 4 g, Sugars: 13 g, Protein: 13 g, Sodium:
66 mg, Cholesterol: 0 mg

Peach Berry Pleasure Smoothie

Always choose organic strawberries because they take in a great deal of the pesticides if they are not grown organically. Strawberries are amazing because of their antioxidants and anti-inflammatory qualities. They have been shown to prevent cardiovascular disease, improve blood sugars, and prevent certain cancers. They should be a part of your weekly diet. Makes 2 servings of 8 ounces each.

1/2 cup frozen of strawberries

1/2 cup frozen of peaches

1/2 of a medium banana

1/3 - 1/2 cup of rice milk (or other milk alternative)

1/2 cup of peach nectar (or apple juice)

1/4 cup of almond butter

1/2 teaspoon of agave

In a blender, add all ingredients and blend for 1 minute. Enjoy!

Prep time: 5 minutes

Nutrients per serving: Calories: 179, Total Fat: 6 g, Sat. Fat: 1 g, Carbs: 33, g, Fiber: 3 g, Sugars: 18 g, Protein: 2 g, Sodium: 24 mg, Cholesterol: 0 mg

Strawberry Banana Surprise Smoothie

Surprise! This smoothie has lettuce in it! The combination of fruit and vegetables gives you vitamin C and fiber. Increased fiber content is essential for proper elimination, detoxification and anti-aging. The almond milk adds healthy monounsaturated fats to this smoothie. Makes 2 servings of 12 ounces each.

1 cup of frozen strawberries

1 frozen banana

2 Romaine lettuce leaves

1/2 cup of almond milk

1/2 cup of water

Add all ingredients to a blender and combine until smooth, about 1 minute.

Prep time: 5 minutes

Nutrients per serving: Calories: 79, Total Fat: 1 g, Sat. Fat: 0 g, Carbs: 18 g, Fiber: 3 g, Sugars: 11 g, Protein: 2 g, Sodium: 39 mg, Cholesterol: 0 mg

Blueberry Antioxidant Blast Smoothie

There is new research showing that blueberries are not damaged when they are frozen. This is great news for people like me who love making smoothies all year around. In addition to high antioxidant content, blueberries help balance blood sugar levels making them perfect for all chronic diseases, including diabetes. The twist in this smoothie is the green tea which supports proper elimination, detoxification and anti-aging. Makes 2 servings of 12 ounces each.

1 cup of frozen blueberries

1 frozen banana

1/2 cup of almond nut butter

1 cup almond milk

1 cup of green tea

*1/2 teaspoon of agave nectar optional

Add all ingredients to a blender and combine until smooth, about 1 minute.

Prep time: 5 minutes

Nutrients per serving: Calories: 140, Total Fat: 6 g, Sat. Fat: 1 g, Carbs: 36 g, Fiber: 6 g, Sugars: 15 g, Protein: 11 g, Sodium: 83 mg, Cholesterol: 0 mg

"If you don't take care of your body,
where are you going to live?"
~Unknown

Almond Milk

Almonds are high in monosaturated fats that are good for your health. These good oils have been shown to lower bad cholesterol. It is also high in vitamin E, magnesium and potassium--all essential for heart health and proper cell metabolism. Make 6 servings.

1/2 cup of almonds
1 cup of filtered water
4 dates, pitted
1 teaspoon of cinnamon

1/2 teaspoon of vanilla extract
1/2 nutmeg, freshly grated
1 teaspoon of coconut oil

1. Rinse almonds and place them in the filtered water to soak for a few hours or overnight.
2. Drain the almonds; place then in a blender or Vitamix for 1 1/2 minutes.
3. Strain the almonds particles from the liquid. Place liquid back in the blender or Vitamix.
4. Add the dates, cinnamon, vanilla, nutmeg and coconut oil to the blender or Vitamix and start low and slowly turn it up until you get to high speed. Continue to blend for another 1 1/2 minutes.
5. Chill for at least 1 hour. Serve.

Prep time: 5 minutes then overnight
Total time 10 minutes

Nutrients per serving: Calories: 149, Total Fat: 7 g, Sat. Fat: 1 g, Carbs: 21 g, Fiber: 3 g, Sugars: 17 g, Protein: 3 g, Sodium: 3 mg, Cholesterol: 0 mg

"The greatest wealth is Health."
~Unknown

Carrot Apple Fresh Juice

Carrot apple juice is one of sweetest fresh fruit and vegetable combinations. A study from the Netherlands showed that yellow and orange colored foods like carrots are protective from heart disease. Combine that with the antioxidants in apples to create a potent fresh juice. Makes 10 ounces.

4-5 carrots, coarsely chopped   1 apple, coarsely chopped

Cut into slices that will fit into your juicer and juice. Drink immediately.
To store, put in an airtight mason jar and refrigerate. Will last for up to 24 hours.

Prep time: 5 minutes

Nutrients per serving: Calories: 195, Total Fat: 1 g, Sat. Fat: 0 g, Carbs: 49 g, Fiber: 11 g, Sugars: 11 g, Protein: 3 g, Sodium: 170 mg, Cholesterol: 0 mg

Apple Cucumber Ginger Fresh Juice

Cucumber extracts have been shown to have both antioxidant and anti-inflammatory properties. These properties are important for all chronic disease and to reverse aging. Ginger is a powerful digestive herb that has anti-inflammatory properties as well. Makes 10 ounces.

1 cucumber, coarsely chopped   2 apples, coarsely chopped
1 inch of ginger

Cut ingredients into slices that will fit into your juicer and juice. Drink immediately. To store, put in an airtight mason jar and refrigerate. Will last for up to 24 hours.

Prep time: 5 minutes

Nutrients per serving: Calories: 224, Total Fat: 1 g, Sat. Fat: 0 g, Carbs: 57 g, Fiber: 11 g, Sugars: 42 g, Protein: 3 g, Sodium: 9 mg, Cholesterol: 0 mg

Pink Lady Fresh Juice

Beets are surprisingly sweet! Most people are afraid of beets, but they are a fabulous food for detoxification and antioxidant support. The phytonutrients in beets, called betalains, are most powerful when eaten raw or in this case juiced. Ginger always adds a wonderful pungent flavor that aids digestion.
Makes 12 ounces.

1/2 beet, coarsely chopped   1 apple, coarsely chopped
4-5 carrots, coarsely chopped   1 inch ginger

Cut ingredients into slices that will fit into your juicer and juice. Drink immediately. To store, put in an airtight mason jar and refrigerate. Will last for up to 24 hours.

Prep time: 5 minutes

Nutrients per serving: Calories: 216, Total Fat: 1 g, Sat. Fat: 0 g, Carbs: 53 g, Fiber: 12 g, Sugars: 33 g, Protein: 3 g, Sodium: 203 mg, Cholesterol: 0 mg

Cool As A Cucumber Fresh Juice

Cucumbers have vitamin C, beta-carotene, and manganese. These antioxidants are responsible for protecting and restoring cells. Makes 10 ounces.

1 cucumber   1 lime, peeled

Cut ingredients into slices that will fit into your juicer and juice. Drink immediately. To store put in an airtight mason jar and refrigerate. Will last for up to 24 hours.

Prep time: 5 minutes

Nutrients per serving: Calories: 54, Total Fat: 1 g, Sat. Fat: 0 g, Carbs: 13 g, Fiber: 4 g, Sugars: 5 g, Protein: 2 g, Sodium: 7 mg, Cholesterol: 0 mg

Kale Pear Mint Fresh Juice

Kale is one of the cruciferous vegetables that are recommended for consumption two to three times every week.
Kale has at least 45 antioxidant flavonoids & phytonutrients, so it supports heart health and has anti-aging properties.
This is one of the thicker juices because of the fiber.
The consistency is more like a smoothie. Makes 12 ounces.

2 cups of kale leaves, tightly packed and coarsely chopped

1 cup of mint, coarsely chopped

2 pears, coarsely chopped

Cut into slices that will fit into your juicer.
Alternate adding the leaves followed by the pears to maximize your juice.
Drink immediately.
To store, put in an airtight mason jar and refrigerate. Will last for up to 24 hours.

Prep time: 5 minutes

Nutrients per serving: Calories: 251, Total Fat: 3 g, Sat. Fat: 1 g, Carbs: 55 g, Fiber: 23 g, Sugars: 15 g, Protein: 12 g, Sodium: 126 mg, Cholesterol: 0 mg

Kale Orange Strawberry Fresh Juice

This is an antioxidant booster juice. It has antioxidants from the kale, oranges and strawberries. Nutrients like vitamin C and quercetin support the reduction of chronic diseases like cancer, heart disease, and obesity. Makes 12 ounces.

1 cup of kale
2 oranges peeled

1 cup of strawberries

Cut the ingredients into slices that will fit into your juicer.
Alternate putting the leaves followed by the oranges and strawberries to maximize your juice.
Drink immediately.
To store, put in an airtight mason jar and refrigerate. Will last for up to 24 hours.

Prep time: 5 minutes

Nutrients per serving: Calories: 172, Total Fat: 1 g, Sat. Fat: 0 g, Carbs: 41 g, Fiber: 9 g, Sugars: 25 g, Protein: 5 g, Sodium: 30 mg, Cholesterol: 0 mg

Cucumber Mint Lime Fresh Juice

This combination of herbs with cucumber and lime is a cool refreshing treat. Cucumber extracts have both antioxidant and anti-inflammatory properties which is important for reducing all chronic disease and to reverse aging. Makes 10 ounces.

1 cucumber

1 cup of mint, tightly packed

1 cup of cilantro, tightly packed

1/2 lime peeled

1/4 jalapeno pepper

Cut into slices that will fit into your juicer.
Alternate putting the leaves followed by the cucumber to maximize your juice.
Drink immediately.
To store, put in an airtight mason jar and refrigerate. Will last for up to 24 hours.

Prep time: 5 minutes

Nutrients per serving: Calories: 144, Total Fat: 2 g, Sat. Fat: 0 g, Carbs: 29 g, Fiber: 18 g, Sugars: 5 g, Protein: 9 g, Sodium: 75 mg, Cholesterol: 0 mg

Kale Celery Cucumber Apple Fresh Juice

This combination of kale, celery, cucumbers and apples reduces inflammation. The reduction of inflammation is important in chronic diseases like heart disease and cancer prevention, so drink up. Makes 12 ounces.

2 cups of kale leaves, tightly packed, coarsely chopped

4 celery stalks, coarsely chopped

1 green apple, coarsely chopped

1 cucumber, coarsely chopped

1/2 inch of ginger

1 lemon peeled

Cut into slices that will fit into your juicer and juice. Drink immediately. To store, put in an airtight mason jar and refrigerate. Will last for up to 24 hours.

Prep time: 5 minutes

Nutrients per serving: Calories: 216, Total Fat: 2 g, Sat. Fat: 0 g, Carbs: 50 g, Fiber: 12 g, Sugars: 25 g, Protein: 7 g, Sodium: 192 mg, Cholesterol: 0 mg

Spinach Lemonade

A little green lemonade anyone?
This is a great way to have some nutrient dense lemonade
with no sugar added! The chlorophyll in the spinach acts as
a refresher and detoxifier for the cells.
This is a shot of juice.
The recipe makes about 4 ounces instead of 8 ounces.

1 green or tart apple, coarsely chopped

1 red or sweet apple, coarsely chopped

1 lemon, peeled

2 cups of spinach

Cut apples into slices that will fit into your juicer.
Alternate putting the leaves followed by the apples to maximize your juice.
Drink immediately.
To store, put in an airtight mason jar and refrigerate. Will last for up to 24 hours.
If you have a Vitamix, here is an adaptation that I think is perfect.
1 red or sweet apples, coarsely chopped
1/2 lemon, peeled
2 cups of spinach
12 ounces of water
Start at a low speed and increase until you reach the high speed. Continue for 30 seconds. Enjoy!

Prep time: 5 minutes

Nutrients per serving: Calories: 217, Total Fat: 1 g, Sat. Fat: 0 g, Carbs: 57 g, Fiber: 9 g, Sugars: 39 g, Protein: 3 g, Sodium: 150 mg, Cholesterol: 0 mg

"Take care of your body.
It's the only place you have to live."
~Jim Rohn

Cinnamon Almond Butter Smoothie

Nuts get a bad rap because they are known for their fat content. Almonds provide protection from heart disease and diabetes by keeping blood sugar levels balanced and reducing high sugar spikes after meals.
Makes 2 servings of 8 ounces each.

1 cup of almond milk

1 frozen banana

1 tablespoon of almond nut
  butter

1 teaspoon of cinnamon

In a blender add almond milk, banana, almond butter and cinnamon. Blend for one minute. Serve.

Prep time: 5 minutes

Nutrients per serving: Calories: 134, Total Fat: 6 g, Sat. Fat: 1 g, Carbs: 20 g, Fiber: 3 g, Sugars: 11 g, Protein: 2 g, Sodium: 72 mg, Cholesterol: 0 mg

"A good laugh and a long sleep are the best cures in the doctor's book."
~Irish Proverb

 # NOTES

Satisfying Soups

Basic Veggie Stock

The nice part about making stock is that you can use all the parts of the vegetables. Throw in roots, stems and all. The nutrients transfer from the vegetables into the broth so it is a nutrient dense way to get your nutrition. Use as many organic vegetables as possible to make this a healing broth. Broth is one of the easiest ways to get nutrients which makes this broth perfect for anyone with digestive issues. It's also a great way to get your energy level up after a cold or flu. Makes 8 servings.

2 tablespoons of extra virgin olive oil

1 cup of yellow onion

2 cups of zucchini

1 cup of carrots

1 1/3 cups of celery

1 potato

1 cup of dried mushrooms

1 cup of parsley

8 garlic cloves

2 bay leaves

1/2 teaspoon of dried thyme

1/2 teaspoon of sage

1 cup of scallions

1 teaspoon of peppercorns

1 teaspoon of sea salt

6 cups of water

1. Coarsely chop the vegetables.
2. In a large soup pot, add the vegetables.
3. Cover the vegetables with water and bring to a boil.
4. Simmer for 45 minutes.
3. Strain the vegetables and discard.
Prep time: 8 minutes
Cook time: 45 minutes

Nutrients per serving: Calories: 185, Total Fat: 4 g, Sat. Fat: 1 g, Carbs: 38 g, Fiber: 6 g, Sugars: 4 g, Protein: 5 g, Sodium: 102 mg, Cholesterol: 0 mg

"Health is a relationship between you and your body"
~Terri Guillemets

Very Veggie Udon Soup

I love soups! This delicious soup includes buckwheat instead of wheat, so everyone including people with wheat sensitivities or those who are gluten-free can enjoy it. There are many immune-boosting ingredients in this soup--like mushrooms, bok choy and onions--that reduce cancer risk. Makes 8 servings.

2 tablespoons of fresh ginger, peeled and sliced

4-5 garlic cloves, crushed

5 cups of vegetable broth

2 teaspoons of extra virgin olive oil

1 3/4 cup (4 ounces) of shiitake or oyster mushrooms, stemmed and sliced

1 cup of red onions, sliced

1 cup of carrots, grated

1/4 teaspoon of crushed red pepper, or to taste

1 small bok choy, sliced

4 ounces of buckwheat udon noodles

1 teaspoon of toasted sesame oil

Rice vinegar to taste

2 teaspoons of Bragg's Liquid Aminos or soy sauce

Garnish:

1/4 cup of chopped scallions

3 teaspoons of sesame seeds

1/2 cup of bean sprouts

1. Put ginger and garlic in a stock pot with broth and bring to a gentle boil.
2. Simmer for 12-15 minutes. Remove ginger and garlic.
3. Add noodles to the stock; cook on low heat for about 8 minutes.
4. In a saucepan add oil, mushrooms, red onions, carrots and crushed red pepper; cook for about 3 minutes.
5. Add bok choy and cook another 2 minutes.
6. Add the mushroom mixture to the stock pot. Simmer for 3 minutes.
7. Add sesame oil, vinegar and Braggs Liquid Aminos to taste.
8. Garnish with scallions, sesame seeds and sprouts.

Prep time: 8 minutes
Cook time: 28 minutes

Nutrients per serving: Calories: 352, Total Fat: 29 g, Sat. Fat: 4 g, Carbs: 22 g, Fiber: 4 g, Sugars: 4 g, Protein: 5 g, Sodium: 381 mg, Cholesterol: 0 mg

Comforting Carrot Soup

This simple carrot soup is perfect for any occasion.
Carrots have been studied specifically for their anti-oxidant
benefits in cardiovascular, or heart health. There is also some
research to support that they can lower the risk of damage from
glaucoma. For an added bonus add two parsnips as well.
Makes 8 servings.

2 tablespoons of olive oil
1/2 jalapeño pepper, seeded and chopped (Keep the seeds for extra heat)
5-6 carrots, sliced
2 parsnips, sliced*
1 yellow onion, sliced
1/2 teaspoon of thyme

1/8 teaspoon of nutmeg
1/4 teaspoon of pepper
1 bay leaf
2 cups of vegetable stock
2 cups of rice milk or other milk alternative
1 tablespoon dill
*optional

1. Place olive oil in the pan on medium heat. Add jalapeño, carrots, parsnips, onions, thyme, nutmeg, pepper and bay leaf.
2. Stir and coat vegetables with seasonings for 1-2 minutes.
3. Add vegetable stock and bring to a boil. Let cook at a slow boil until the vegetables are tender, about 30 minutes.
4. Remove bay leaf and discard.
5. Remove vegetable mixture from the pot and puree with rice milk in the blender or food processor until smooth.
6. Return to the pan and cook 2 minutes until warm.
7. Serve with the dill as a garnish.

Prep time: 10 minutes
Cook time: 35 minutes

Nutrients per serving: Calories: 114, Total Fat: 6 g, Sat. Fat: 1 g, Carbs: 19 g, Fiber: 5 g, Sugars: 5 g, Protein: 1 g, Sodium: 194 mg, Cholesterol: 0 mg

"All you need is love. But a little chocolate now
and then doesn't hurt."
Charles M. Schulz

Fantastically Fresh Tomato Soup

I grew up eating canned tomato soup, but this is so much better! Tomatoes have a phytonutrient called lycopene that has been associated with bone health. The interesting thing about lycopene is that it increases when tomatoes are cooked. This lovely soup provides an extra serving of lycopene which reduces your risk for prostate cancer. It also increases your heart health with each bite. Makes 8 servings.

1 tablespoon of extra virgin olive oil

6 garlic cloves, crushed

1/2 cup of yellow onions, chopped

6 yellow tomatoes or plum tomatoes, chopped

2 cups of organic vegetable broth

1 cup of corn kernels

1 cup of red or yellow bell peppers, chopped

1 jalapeño pepper, chopped

1/2 teaspoon of lemon zest, grated

1/2 teaspoon of sea salt

1/2 teaspoon of black pepper

1 teaspoon of apple cider vinegar

1 tablespoon of fresh basil, chopped

1 tablespoon of fresh parsley, chopped

1 tablespoon of fresh chives, chopped

1. In a saucepan, add olive oil, garlic and onions. Sauté for 2 minutes.
2. Add tomatoes, vegetable broth, corn, bell peppers, jalapeño, lemon zest, salt, black pepper and apple cider vinegar; bring to a boil, about 5 minutes.
3. Remove from heat. Place soup in the food processor along with basil, parsley and chives; blend for 30 seconds to 1 minute.

Prep time: 10 minutes
Cook time: 7 minutes

Nutrients per serving: Calories: 59, Total Fat: 2 g, Sat. Fat: 0 g, Carbs: 10 g, Fiber: 2 g, Sugars: 3 g, Protein: 2 g, Sodium: 105 mg, Cholesterol: 0 mg

Green Split Pea Soup

Split pea soup is an easy, quick soup that can be made in just about 30 minutes. Split peas are a source of protein, so they help to stabilize blood sugar for diabetics and those with pre-diabetes. The fiber in split peas help with digestive and heart issues. Makes 8 servings.

2 teaspoons of olive oil

2 carrots, diced

2 stalks of celery, diced

1 small onion, diced

1 bay leaf

5 garlic cloves, minced

1 pinch of cayenne pepper

2 cups of green split peas, washed

4 cups of vegetable broth

4 cups of water

1 teaspoon of sea salt

Juice of 1 lemon

1. In a soup pot, add oil, carrots, celery, onion, bay leaf, garlic cloves and cayenne pepper; sauté for 5 minutes.
2. In a strainer, wash the split peas 3-4 times under cold water or until the water is no longer dirty.
3. Add split peas, vegetable broth and water; bring to a boil.
4. Once the broth is boiling, turn down to simmer with the lid on.
5. Let cook for 20 minutes.
6. Add salt and cook for another 5 minutes.
7. Add lemon juice to taste.
8. Serve.

Prep time: 10 minutes
Cook time: 25 minutes

Nutrients per serving: Calories: 90, Total Fat: 1 g, Sat. Fat: 0 g, Carbs: 16 g, Fiber: 5 g, Sugars: 4 g, Protein: 5 g, Sodium: 285 mg, Cholesterol: 0 mg

"Don't let what you cannot do interfere with what you can do"
~ UCLA basketball coach John Wooden,
one of the winnest coaches in America

Curry Pumpkin Soup

This is one of my favorite soups for the fall. I love roasting a small pumpkin and using the meat for this soup.
Pumpkins are a source of unsaturated fat, antioxidants and fiber making them perfect for regulating cholesterol and heart issues. They also aid in cancer prevention.
The coconut milk and curry are both supportive to the digestive tract and can reduce digestive issues.
You can roast the seeds from the pumpkin and have them for a healthy snack or to garnish the soup. Makes 8 servings.

1 tablespoon of olive oil

1/2 cup of yellow onions, chopped

4 garlic cloves, crushed

1/2 teaspoon of sea salt

1 tablespoon of curry powder

1/2 teaspoon of cumin

1 1/2 tablespoon of ginger, grated

1/4 teaspoon of nutmeg, ground

2 cups of pureed pumpkin or tightly packed pumpkin

3/4 cup of coconut milk

2 cups of vegetable broth

1 cup of water

1. In a soup pot, add oil, onion, garlic, salt, curry powder, cumin, ginger and nutmeg.
2. Sauté on medium heat for 4 minutes or until onions are translucent.
3. Stir in pumpkin, coconut milk, vegetable broth and water.
4. Reduce to a simmer for 15 minutes.
5. Place in a blender and puree for 1 minute.
6. Serve.

Prep time: 10 minutes
Cook time: 20 minutes

Nutrients per serving: Calories: 81, Total Fat: 7 g, Sat. Fat: 4 g, Carbs: 6 g, Fiber: 1 g, Sugars: 1 g, Protein: 1 g, Sodium: 203 mg, Cholesterol: 0 mg

Green Lentil Soup

Green lentils are very versatile and can be made into a soup or a lentil salad. This is a simple recipe that takes about 30 minutes. Lentils have both sources of protein and soluble fiber that promote the lowering of cholesterol levels and helps with satiety at the same time.
The pistachio cream dollop on top gives the soup a wonderful creamy rich quality. Makes 8 servings.

Pistachio Cream

1/2 cup of pistachios

1 teaspoon of fresh squeezed lemon juice

2 tablespoons of water

1/4 teaspoon of agave nectar

Green Lentil Soup

2 teaspoons of extra virgin olive oil

2 carrots, diced

1 small onion, diced

1 bay leaf

5 garlic cloves, minced

1 pinch of cayenne pepper

2 cups of green lentils, washed

4 cups of vegetable broth

4 cups of water

1 teaspoon of sea salt

Juice of 1/2 lemon

Pistachio Cream

1. Place all ingredients in the blender.
2. Blend until smooth, about 1 minute.

Green Lentil Soup

1. In a soup pot, add oil, carrots, onion, bay leaf, garlic cloves and cayenne pepper; sauté for 5 minutes.
2. In a strainer, wash the lentils 3-4 times under cold water or until the water is no longer dirty.
3. Add lentils, vegetable broth and water; bring to a boil.
4. Once the broth is boiling, turn down to simmer with the lid on.
5. Let cook for 20 minutes.
6. While the soup is simmering prepare the pistachio cream.
7. Add salt and cook for another 10 minutes.
8. Add lemon juice to taste.
9. Ladle 1 cup into a bowl.
10. Add a dollop of pistachio cream to the top of the bowl. Serve.

Prep time: 5 minutes
Cook time: 35 minutes

Nutrients per serving: Calories: 87, Total Fat: 1 g, Sat. Fat: 9 g, Carbs: 15 g, Fiber: 5 g, Sugars: 3 g, Protein: 5 g, Sodium: 300 mg, Cholesterol: 0 mg

Roasted Butternut Squash Soup

*This is a soup-er simple recipe that takes minutes to make
after you finish roasting the butternut squash in the oven.
Butternut squash is high in beta carotene and vitamin C. Beta
carotene--the pre-cursor to vitamin A--is essential for cell repair.
Antioxidant and anti-inflammatory properties are found in this
delicious soup as well. Makes 8 servings.*

6 cups of butternut squash,
peeled and diced -
approximately 1 butternut
squash

1 tablespoon of extra virgin
olive oil

1/2 teaspoon of sea salt

1/2 teaspoon of fresh ground
pepper

1/2 teaspoon of fresh ground
nutmeg

6 cups of vegetable broth

1/2 teaspoon of maple syrup

1/2 teaspoon of ground
cinnamon

1/4 teaspoon of coriander

1/4 teaspoon of ground
ginger

1/2 teaspoon of fresh
squeezed lemon juice

1. Preheat the oven to 375 °F
2. Cover a cookie sheet with parchment paper.
3. In a bowl, toss the squash, extra virgin olive oil, salt, pepper
and nutmeg until well coated.
4. Place the squash on parchment paper and bake for 40-50
minutes until the squash is tender.
5. Put butternut squash in the blender along with the vegetable
broth, maple syrup, cinnamon, coriander, ginger and lemon
juice.
6. Puree for 2 minutes.
7. Pour the pureed soup into a soup pot and bring to a rolling
boil.
8. Turn off heat and serve.

Prep time: 10 minutes
Bake time: 50 minutes
Cook time: 10 minutes

Nutrients per serving: Calories: 76, Total Fat: 2 g, Sat. Fat: 0 g,
Carbs: 16 g, Fiber: 5 g, Sugars: 4 g, Protein: 1 g, Sodium: 400
mg, Cholesterol: 0 mg

Pink Lentil Soup

I learned to make lentils with my Indian friends in naturopathic medical school. Lentils are a source of protein and soluble fiber that's quick and easy to prepare. Turmeric, an herb most studied for its anti-inflammatory properties, is one of the stars of this soup. It is fantastic for all chronic diseases--diabetes, heart disease and obesity. The other herbs are warming and support digestion, so this soup is pleasing to the palate and the tummy. Makes 8 servings.

1 cup of pink lentils

4 cups of water

1/2 fresh squeezed lemon

Salt to taste

2 teaspoons of ghee or olive oil

1/4 teaspoon of ground cumin

4 teaspoons of ginger, grated

1/4 teaspoon turmeric

1/4 teaspoon of coriander

1 cup of tomatoes, diced

3 cloves of garlic, crushed

Dash hot chili powder

1. Rinse pink lentils under cold water 3-4 times or until the water is no longer dirty.
2. In a 4 quart pan, add lentils and water. Bring water to a boil; then reduce to a simmer for 20 -25 minutes or until soft.
3. Add lemon and salt.
4. While the lentils are cooking get another small sauce pan and place it on low heat.
5. Add ghee or olive oil, cumin, ginger, turmeric and coriander; sauté about 2 minutes.
6. Add tomatoes, crushed garlic, and chili powder. Turn off the heat.
8. Finally, add the contents of the sauce pan to the lentils and serve as a soup.
9. Makes a great dish served with rice.

Prep time: 5 minutes
Cook time: 27 minutes

Nutrients per serving: Calories: 95, Total Fat: 3 g, Sat. Fat: 0 g, Carbs: 14 g, Fiber: 5 g, Sugars: 2 g, Protein: 5 g, Sodium: 130 mg, Cholesterol: 0 mg

Spice It Up Gazpacho Soup

I was not a fan of cold soups, but this one changed my mind! Tomatoes have been shown to help lower cholesterol and triglycerides. They also help to prevent platelets from sticking together. These benefits are extremely important for anyone with a history of heart disease. Makes 8 servings.

3 ripe tomatoes, chopped

1/4 cup of red onion, finely chopped

1/2 cup of cucumber, peeled, seeded, chopped

1/2 cup of red pepper, seeded and chopped

1/2 cup of celery, finely chopped

1 tablespoon of fresh parsley, chopped

2 tablespoons of fresh chives, chopped

2 garlic cloves, minced

1/4 cup of red wine vinegar

1/4 cup of extra virgin olive oil

2 cups of tomato juice

Juice of 1/2 lemon, freshly squeezed

1/8 teaspoon of sea salt

1/8 teaspoon of freshly ground pepper

1/8 teaspoon of red pepper chili flakes

1/8 teaspoon of cayenne pepper

1. Add all ingredients to a blender or Vitamix.
2. Blend to desired consistency, about 1 minute and 30 seconds.
3. Serve immediately or chill and let flavors blend.

Prep time 15 minutes

Nutrients per serving: Calories: 86, Total Fat: 7 g, Sat. Fat: 1 g, Carbs: 5 g, Fiber: 1 g, Sugars: 3 g, Protein: 1 g, Sodium: 42 mg, Cholesterol: 0 mg

"Let food be thy medicine and medicine be thy food."
~ Hippocrates

Black Bean Chili

This will become a family favorite for a chilly fall or winter night! The nutrients that give black beans their dark color also make them a great antioxidant and anti-inflammatory food. Anti-oxidants neutralize chemicals that damage our cells, cause aging and increase our risk of heart disease and diabetes. The more antioxidants in our diets, the better it is for our health. Makes 10 servings.

2 tablespoons of extra virgin olive oil

1 cup of yellow onion, chopped

1 cup of red bell pepper, chopped

2 tablespoons of garlic, minced

1 medium zucchini, diced

1 medium eggplant, diced

2 cups of corn kernels (fresh or frozen)

5 large Portobello mushrooms, cubed

1 tablespoon of chili powder

1 tablespoon of ground cumin

1 1/4 teaspoon of sea salt

Pinch of cayenne pepper, or to taste

4 large tomatoes, peeled, seeded and chopped

3 cups of cooked black beans (two 15 ounce cans)

1 can of crushed tomatoes (15 ounces)

1 cup of vegetable stock (check label for gluten-free)

1. In a large pot, heat the oil over medium-high heat. Add the onions, bell peppers and garlic; cook about 3 minutes.

2. Add the zucchini, eggplant, corn and mushrooms; stir until soft, about 5-6 minutes.

3. Add the chili powder, cumin, salt and cayenne; cook about 30 seconds.

4. Add the tomatoes, beans, crush tomatoes and vegetable stock; stir well.

5. Bring to a boil. Reduce the heat to medium-low and simmer for about 20 minutes, stirring occasionally.

Prep time: 20 minutes
Cook time: 30 minutes

Nutrients per serving: Calories: 188, Total Fat: 4 g, Sat. Fat: 1 g, Carbs: 34 g, Fiber: 12 g, Sugars: 6 g, Protein: 9 g, Sodium: 390 mg, Cholesterol: 0 mg

Velvety Beet Soup

Beets are an under-utilized vegetable that can be very versatile.
Beets are a great food to help remove toxins from your body.
The deep reddish/purple/orange color is indicative of their
antioxidant potency. The antioxidants support the repair and
restorations of cells. This helps our bodies heal all diseases
from colds to cancer. Makes 8 servings.

6 red beets

2 tablespoons of extra virgin olive oil

1 teaspoon of fresh ginger

1/4 teaspoon of salt

1/4 teaspoon of fresh black pepper

6 cups of vegetable broth

1 teaspoon of fresh squeezed lemon juice

1. Preheat the oven to 400 °F.
2. Place parchment paper on a baking sheet; set aside.
3. Wash beets and peel them.
4. Cut them into 1-inch slices; place them in a large bowl.
5. Add the olive oil, ginger, salt and pepper; toss to coat all the pieces well.
6. Place the beets on parchment paper; roast for 40 minutes.
7. Place the beets in blender along with 3 cups of the vegetable broth; puree until smooth.
8. Pour the soup into a soup pan with the additional 3 cups of vegetable broth. Cook for 5 minutes or until warm.
9. Add the lemon juice to taste and serve.

Prep time: 5 minutes
Bake time: 40 minutes
Cook time: 5 minutes

Nutrients per serving: Calories: 89, Total Fat: 5 g, Sat. Fat: 1 g, Carbs: 11 g, Fiber: 2 g, Sugars: 8 g, Protein: 1 g, Sodium: 500 mg, Cholesterol: 0 mg

Cooking is like love.
It should be entered into with abandon or not at all
~ Harriet Von Horne

Spectacularly Simple Salads

Basic Salad Dressing

Salad dressings are so easy to make. After you have made your first batch you will wonder why you hadn't discovered how to make salad dressing earlier. The advantage of making your own salad dressing is that you have control over the ingredients. The trans-fatty acids and extra sugars found in most bottled dressing are absent from this delicious recipe. Salad dressing and marinades have four basic tastes: a fat, an acid, a sweet and a salt. You can use this basic recipe and add fresh or dried herbs to change or enhance this basic recipe. Makes 8 servings.

3 tablespoons of your favorite vinegar

1/2 cup of extra virgin olive oil

1 pinch of salt

1 pinch of pepper

1/2 teaspoon of maple syrup

Mix all ingredients together and pour over salad.

Prep time: 5 minutes

Nutrients per serving: Calories: 63, Total Fat: 7 g, Sat. Fat: 1 g, Carbs: 0 g, Fiber: 0 g, Sugars: 0 g, Protein: 0 g, Sodium: 59 mg, Cholesterol: 0 mg

Lemon Citrus Dressing

This lovely, light lemon dressing is great for any salad or marinade. In this dressing we are using lemon juice instead of vinegar. The lemon juice is acidic so it works just as perfectly. Lemons have antioxidant and anti-cancer properties, so even in your salad dressing you get benefits that help rejuvenate and support healthy cells. Makes 6 servings.

Juice of a lemon, squeezed

1/2 cup of extra virgin olive oil

1 pinch of salt

1 pinch of pepper

1/2 teaspoon of maple syrup

Mix all ingredients together and pour over salad.

Prep time: 5 minutes

Nutrients per serving: Calories: 89, Total Fat: 7 g, Sat. Fat: 1 g, Carbs: 0 g, Fiber: 0 g, Sugars: 6 g, Protein: 0 g, Sodium: 59 mg, Cholesterol: 0 mg

Citrus Berry Salad Dressing

If you like fruity vinaigrettes, you will love this smooth pink treat. Strawberries and clementines give this dressing a tangy taste packed with vitamin C for an immune system boost! Vitamin C neutralizes free radicals and helps to prevent the development and progression of blood vessel disease and diabetic heart disease. Makes 6 servings.

6 fresh strawberries

1/2 of a fresh clementine

1/4 cup of safflower oil

1/2 teaspoon of ground ginger

A few pieces of crystallized ginger (optional)

2 tablespoons rice wine vinegar

2 cups of mixed field greens

1. In a blender, mix strawberries, clementine, oil, ground ginger, crystallized ginger and vinegar for 30-45 seconds.
2. Pour over salad greens and serve.
* If you don't have fresh clementines, you can use 1/4 cup of canned clementine pieces.

Prep time: 5 minutes

Nutrients per serving: Calories: 95, Total Fat: 9 g, Sat. Fat: 1 g, Carbs: 3 g, Fiber: 1 g, Sugars: 2 g, Protein: 0 g, Sodium: 1 mg, Cholesterol: 0 mg

"The food you eat can either be the safest and most powerful form of medicine or the slowest form of poison."
~Ann Wigmore, cofounder of Hippocrates Health Institute

Lime Mint Cilantro Dressing

This is an example of how you can use your favorite herbs to boost the flavor of a salad dressing. Cilantro is considered an anti-diabetic and anti-inflammatory herb. Lime has phytochemicals called flavonoids that have been shown to stop cancer cells from developing. Makes 6 servings.

1/2 of a fresh squeezed lime juice

1/4 cup of fresh cilantro finely chopped

8 fresh mint leaves

1/4 cup of extra virgin olive oil

1/4 teaspoon of agave

Pinch of sea salt

Pinch pepper

You can make this one of two ways.

Option #1

You can whisk all the ingredients together to create this lovely dressing.

Option #2

1. In a blender, mix lime juice, cilantro, mint, oil, agave, salt and pepper.

2. Blend until smooth, about 1 minute. Taste and adjust as needed.

Prep time: 5 minutes

Nutrients per serving: Calories: 122, Total Fat: 10 g, Sat. Fat: 1 g, Carbs: 8 g, Fiber: 2 g, Sugars: 3 g, Protein: 2 g, Sodium: 99 mg, Cholesterol: 0 mg

"The shared meal elevates eating from a mechanical process of fueling the body to a ritual of family and community, from the mere animal biology to an act of culture."
~ Michael Pollan, In Defense of Food: An Eater's Manifesto

Tangy Couscous Salad

This dish was inspired by leftover couscous that I did not want to throw away. Instead, I added summer vegetables and chickpeas to create a meal balanced with fiber and protein that's excellent for balancing blood sugars and heart health. This balanced salad can help you lose weight. It's a super meal that's super-fast to prepare! If you want to make this recipe gluten free, use quinoa instead of couscous. Makes 6 servings.

1/4 cup of extra virgin olive oil

Juice of 1 lemon

1 teaspoon of maple syrup

1 teaspoon of apple cider vinegar

1 teaspoon of dry mustard

1 teaspoon of fresh basil, finely chopped

Pinch of black pepper

Pinch of sea salt

Salad ingredients

1 cup couscous, cooked

1/2 cup of scallions

1/2 cup of carrots, shredded

1/2 cup of celery, chopped

1/2 cup of cucumber, washed, seeded and cut into cubes

1 cup of cooked chickpeas

1. In an air-tight container, combine olive oil, lemon juice, maple syrup, apple cider vinegar, mustard, basil, salt and pepper.
2. Shake well.
1. In a bowl, add couscous, scallions, carrots, celery cucumbers, and chickpeas.
2. Pour dressing over salad and toss.
*If you need to prepare the couscous here is a simple way to make it!

Couscous preparation
1. Bring 1 cup of water to a boil.
2. Add 1 cup of couscous.
3. Cover with a lid and let stand for 5-10 minutes or until the water as absorbed.
4. Fluff and let stand.

Prep time: 10 minutes
Cook Time 12 minutes

Nutrients per serving: Calories: 176, Total Fat: 10 g, Sat. Fat: 1 g, Carbs: 19 g, Fiber: 3 g, Sugars: 2 g, Protein: 4 g, Sodium: 214 mg, Cholesterol: 0 mg

Stress-Busting Salad

Even though this salad only has 4 ingredients, it's loaded with anti-oxidants and omega-3 fatty acids which is the perfect combination to prevent stress from damaging the cells of the body. This protects our bodies from aging, diabetes, heart disease and other chronic diseases. Makes 6 servings.

Salad ingredients

4 cups of baby spinach

1 small avocado diced

1 small navel orange, cut into slices

1/2 cup of walnuts

Dressing ingredients

4 teaspoons of fresh squeezed orange juice

1/2 teaspoon of orange zest (use an organic orange)

1/2 teaspoon of fresh squeezed lemon juice

2 teaspoons of extra virgin olive oil

1/2 teaspoon of agave nectar

Pinch of salt

1 teaspoon of fresh mint, finely chopped

Ground black pepper

1. In a large bowl, add the spinach. Sprinkle the avocado, orange pieces, and walnuts on top of the spinach leaves.
2. In a small bowl, whisk together orange juice, orange zest, lemon juice, oil, agave, salt and mint.
3. Pour over the salad and lightly toss.
4. Top with fresh ground pepper.

Prep time: 8 minutes

Nutrients per serving: Calories: 189, Total Fat: 15 g, Sat. Fat: 2 g, Carbs: 13 g, Fiber: 5 g, Sugars: 6 g, Protein: 4 g, Sodium: 131 mg, Cholesterol: 0 mg

We all eat and it would be a sad waste of opportunity to eat badly
~Anna Thomas

Two Tomato Salad

*There are so many varieties and flavors of tomatoes.
One of my favorite varieties is the orange sundrop tomato
because they taste like candy. Research shows that certain
antioxidants in tomatoes, like lycopene may be more available
in yellow and orange varieties. Antioxidants and lycopene
help with bone health. Makes 4 servings.*

Dressing ingredients:

1 cup of fresh basil leaves

2 tablespoons of extra virgin olive oil

1 garlic clove

Pinch of sea salt

1/4 cup of pine nuts

2 tablespoons of water

Salad ingredients:

2 cups of lettuce leaves, torn

1/2 cup of sundrop tomatoes, chopped

1/2 cup of cherry tomatoes, chopped

1/2 cup of cucumbers, chopped

1. In a blender, combine basil, oil, garlic, salt, pine nuts and water. Blend for about 45 seconds.
2. Tear lettuce leaves into bite size pieces and arrange on the serving plate. Add the tomatoes and cucumbers in the center of the plate.
3. Pour the dressing over the salad and serve.

Prep time: 10 minutes

Nutrients per serving: Calories: 133, Total Fat: 13 g, Sat. Fat: 1 g, Carbs: 4 g, Fiber: 1 g, Sugars: 2 g, Protein: 2 g, Sodium: 125 mg, Cholesterol: 0 mg

*"The doctor of the future will no longer treat the
human frame with drugs, but rather will cure and
prevent disease with nutrition."*
~Thomas Edison

Garlicky Kale Salad

I consider kale a super food. Kale is a member of the cruciferous vegetable family. This super family has substantial health benefits for fighting disease and prevents damage that leads to cancer. Kale also has quercitin which has anti-inflammatory and antioxidant properties. Other cruciferous family members include broccoli, cauliflower, cabbage and bok choy. Include them in your weekly routine. Makes 4 servings.

1 bunch of raw kale, washed, de-stemmed and dried

2 tablespoons of extra virgin olive oil

2 tablespoons of tahini

2 tablespoons of apple cider vinegar

1/2 teaspoon of cayenne pepper

1 tablespoon of Bragg's liquid amino acids

4 tablespoons of nutritional yeast

2 teaspoons of minced garlic

1/2 teaspoon of agave

2 tablespoons of sesame seeds

1. Break or cut kale into bite size pieces and place in a large bowl.
2. Mix olive oil, tahini, apple cider vinegar, cayenne pepper, Braggs, nutritional yeast, garlic, and agave.
3. Pour dressing over kale; toss until kale is well coated.
4. Cover the salad and let sit in the fridge for at least an hour to marinate. You can prepare up to a day in advance.
5. Sprinkle on some sesame seeds before serving, if so desired.

Prep time: 5 minutes
Chill time: at least 1 hour

Nutrients per serving: Calories: 188, Total Fat: 14 g, Sat. Fat: 2 g, Carbs: 12 g, Fiber: 3 g, Sugars: 1 g, Protein: 5 g, Sodium: 223 mg, Cholesterol: 0 mg

"To insure good health: eat lightly,
breathe deeply, live moderately, cultivate cheerfulness,
and maintain an interest in life."
~William Londen

Wilted Salad with Quinoa

This is a deceptively filling salad. The corn and quinoa give this dish the appearance of a light side salad. All the veggies load it with filling fiber that supports heart health while lowering cholesterol levels. Both the quinoa and chickpeas are good sources of protein, so you have a complete meal in one bowl. This salad is ideal for weight loss and blood sugar balancing.
Makes 6 servings.

1 cup of organic vegetable broth (read label to make sure gluten-free)

1/2 cup of quinoa, rinsed

2 ears of corn or 1/2 cup corn kernels (fresh or frozen)

1/2 cup of snap peas, chopped

1/2 cup of red or green bell pepper, chopped

1/2 cup of cherry tomatoes, halved

1 cup of fresh basil, finely chopped

1/2 teaspoon of sea salt

1/2 teaspoon of black pepper

1 cup of cooked chickpeas (may use canned)

1/4 cup of white wine vinegar

2 garlic cloves, minced

1/3 cup of extra virgin olive oil

1/2 cup of scallions, diced

1. In a 4-quart pan, bring vegetable broth to a boil. Add quinoa, reduce to a simmer, cover and cook until water is absorbed. About 20 minutes.
2. Turn off heat. Wait 5 minutes and fluff with a fork.
3. If using fresh corn, heat enough water to cover the corn cobs and add a pinch of salt. Bring to a boil. Drop corn into the water and cook for 8 minutes. Drain. Cut the kernels of the cob and add to a large bowl.
4. Add quinoa to the bowl. Toss in snap peas, bell peppers, tomatoes, 2/3 cup of basil (reserve 1/3 cup for the dressing), salt, pepper, chickpeas and white wine vinegar.
5. In a small saucepan, heat the oil, garlic, scallions and remaining 1/3 cup of basil.
6. Sauté for 1 minute. Remove from heat and pour over the salad. Serve.

Prep time: 20 minutes
Cook time: 20 minutes

Nutrients per serving: Calories: 213, Total Fat: 11 g, Sat. Fat: 2 g, Carbs: 25 g, Fiber: 4 g, Sugars: 2 g, Protein: 5 g, Sodium: 150 mg, Cholesterol: 0 mg

Asian Cole Slaw

This cole slaw has great oils and big flavors that pair nicely with so many main dishes. Cabbage is a member of the cruciferous vegetable family. Including any of these super foods in your daily diet reduces cancer risk and tissue damage by reducing free radicals. Protecting cells promotes anti-aging.
Makes 6 servings.

1 cup of carrots

2 cups of red cabbage

1 teaspoon of fresh ginger, finely grated

1 teaspoon of Tamari

3/4 to 1 teaspoon of agave

1 teaspoon of toasted sesame oil

3 tablespoons of rice wine vinegar

1 teaspoon of fresh cilantro, chopped

1. Grate the carrots and cabbage together in a bowl.
2. In a separate bowl, whisk together the ginger, tamari, agave, sesame oil, rice wine vinegar and cilantro.
3. Toss the dressing over the carrots and cabbage. Serve.

Prep time: 10 minutes
Chill time: 15 minutes or longer

Nutrients per serving: Calories: 26, Total Fat: 1 g, Sat. Fat: 0 g, Carbs: 4 g, Fiber: 1 g, Sugars: 2 g, Protein: 1 g, Sodium: 75 mg, Cholesterol: 0 mg

"The best of all medicine is resting and fasting"
~Ben Franklin

Orange Rosemary Salad

This is a nice blend of spices and fruit. The jicama is a starchy sweet vegetable that adds a wonderfully mild and crunchy flavor to this salad. If you cannot find jicama, you can use apples as a substitute. The antioxidant properties of vitamin C are important to skin and bone integrity. Vitamin C is a key vitamin for the reduction of stress. Makes 4 servings.

Dressing ingredients:

1/4 cup of extra virgin olive oil

1/4 cup juice - clementine, tangerine or sweet orange

1/2 teaspoon of chopped rosemary leaves

1/8 teaspoon of sea salt

1/8 teaspoon of black pepper

1/8 teaspoon of paprika

1/4 teaspoon of ground mustard

1 tablespoon of red wine vinegar

Salad ingredients:

2 cups mixed salad greens

1 clementine, tangerine or sweet orange, sectioned and chopped

1 cup chopped jicama

1 cup chopped pecans

1. In a small bowl, whisk oil, clementine juice, rosemary, salt, pepper, paprika, mustard and vinegar together.
2. In a large bowl add, salad greens, clementines, jicama, and pecans.
3. Sprinkle with salad dressing and toss lightly.

Prep time: 8 minutes

Nutrients per serving: Calories: 252, Total Fat: 23 g, Sat. Fat: 2 g, Carbs: 11 g, Fiber: 5 g, Sugars: 5 g, Protein: 3 g, Sodium: 66 mg, Cholesterol: 0 mg

"If it came from a plant, eat it; if it was made in a plant, don't. "
~Michael Pollan

Bulgur Wheat Salad

When you're a vegetarian or vegan it is important to vary the grains you eat for flavor and nutrient composition. You can always substitute a gluten-free grain in this lovely salad. Since bulgur is a whole food it has many B vitamins and other nutrients found in the hull. The bell peppers are high in antioxidants that protect cells from damage due to chronic disease. Makes 6 servings.

Salad ingredients:

1 cup of Bulgur wheat

1 cup of boiling water

1/2 cup of red bell peppers, chopped

1/2 cup of yellow peppers, chopped

1/2 cup of orange peppers, chopped

1/2 cup of celery, chopped

1/4 cup of fresh parsley, chopped

1/2 cup of toasted cashews

Dressing ingredients:

1 tablespoon of extra virgin olive oil

2 tablespoons of fresh squeezed lemon juice

1/2 teaspoon of agave nectar

Pinch of sea salt

Pinch of black pepper

1. Rinse bulgur wheat and place in a bowl.
2. Add 1 cup of boiling water to the bowl; let stand for 1 hour.
3. In small separate bowl make the dressing. Whisk together the oil, lemon juice, agave, salt and black pepper.
4. Fluff the bulgur wheat.
5. To the bowl with bulgur, add peppers, celery, parsley, cashews and dressing.
6. Toss ingredients together.

Prep time: 15 minutes

Nutrients per serving: Calories: 117, Total Fat: 3 g, Sat. Fat: 0 g, Carbs: 21 g, Fiber: 5 g, Sugars: 2 g, Protein: 3 g, Sodium: 92 mg, Cholesterol: 0 mg

Fruity Fall Field Salad

Fall is an awesome time for fruits like apples and pears. Apples have a surprising amount of immune stimulating nutrients like quercitin and vitamin C among others. Combining apples and walnuts changes up this salad to stress-busting status! If you want your children to eat more salad try adding more fruit to your salads. You might be surprised at the results. Makes 4 servings.

Dressing Ingredients

2 tablespoons of extra virgin olive oil

2 teaspoons of lemon juice

1 teaspoon of lemon zest (use an organic lemon)

2 teaspoons of walnut oil

2 tablespoons of dill, chopped

Pinch of sea salt to taste

1/4 teaspoon of maple syrup

Salad Ingredients

2 Granny Smith apples, sliced

1/2 cup of chopped walnuts

2 cups of mixed salad greens

1. In a small bowl, whisk olive oil, lemon juice, zest, walnut oil, dill, sea salt and maple syrup into a dressing.
2. In a large bowl, add salad greens, chopped walnuts and sliced apples.
3. Pour salad dressing onto the salad and toss.

Prep time: 8 minutes

Nutrients per serving: Calories: 234, Total Fat: 19 g, Sat. Fat: 2 g, Carbs: 16 g, Fiber: 4 g, Sugars: 10 g, Protein: 5 g, Sodium: 9 mg, Cholesterol: 0 mg

"Health is like money, we never have a true idea of its value until we lose it."
~Josh Billings

Cranberry Pecan Salad

Dried cranberries are starting to become more popular as a staple in the pantry. The beautiful red color of this fruit gives us a hint to its antioxidant and anti-inflammatory properties. These properties protect the heart and immune system. In order to take full advantage of the benefits of dried cranberries, it's best to get the unsweetened ones. Makes 4 servings.

1/4 cup of extra virgin olive oil

2 tablespoons of rice vinegar

2 tablespoons of agave

1/4 teaspoon of sea salt

2 cups of spinach leaves

1/2 cup of red onion, thinly sliced

1/2 cup of dried cranberries

1/2 cup of raw pecans

1. In a small bowl, mix olive oil, rice vinegar, agave, and salt into a dressing.
2. Place pecans in a saucepan over medium high heat for 5 minutes to toast; stirring from time to time.
3. Remove pecans from heat.
4, In a big bowl mix the spinach, red onions and cranberries with pecans.
4. Pour salad dressing and serve.

Prep time: 10 minutes
Cook time: 5 minutes

Nutrients per serving: Calories: 338, Total Fat: 24 g, Sat. Fat: 3 g, Carbs: 33 g, Fiber: 3 g, Sugars: 25 g, Protein: 2 g, Sodium: 157 mg, Cholesterol: 0 mg

"It's bizarre that the produce manager is more important to my children's health than the pediatrician."
~Meryl Streep

Summer's Sensational Salad

What makes this fruit salad fantastic is the citrus dressing! This salad and dressing create an antioxidant bonanza-- which means it is a great recipe to reduce damage to the cells. Strawberries, blueberries, and kiwis have blood sugar stabilizing effects and are a good choice of fruit for diabetics who can handle small amounts of fruit. This salad is high in Vitamin C and other antioxidants so it supports heart health and anti-aging. Makes 8 servings.

2 tablespoons of fresh mint, chopped

1 tablespoon of lemon zest (use an organic lemon)

1 tablespoon of lime zest (use an organic lime)

Juice of 1 orange

Juice of 1 lemon

Juice of 1 lime

1/8 cup of turbinado sugar

1 cup of fresh raspberries

2 peaches, cut into chunks

2 kiwis, cut into chunks

1 clementine or tangerine, peeled and broken into wedges

1 cup of strawberries, cut into chunks

1 cup of blueberries

1 cup of pineapple chunks

1. In a small bowl, whisk the fresh mint, lime zest, lemon zest, lemon juice, orange juice, lime juice and turbinado sugar into a dressing.
2. In a large bowl, mix raspberries, peaches, kiwis, clementines, strawberries, blueberries and pineapple.
3. Pour the dressing over the fruit and refrigerate one hour or until ready to serve.

Prep time: 15 minutes

Nutrients per serving: Calories: 83, Total Fat: 0 g, Sat. Fat: 0 g, Carbs: 21 g, Fiber: 4 g, Sugars: 15 g, Protein: 1 g, Sodium: 2 mg, Cholesterol: 0 mg

On a Mission Fig Salad

The fig is a sweet tasting fruit that doesn't get its proper respect. Not only do figs taste great, but they're fiber rich and have been shown to lower triglyceride levels. They have high levels of potassium and help control blood pressure. This salad also supports heart health and the balancing of blood sugar.
Makes 6 servings.

Ingredients for Salad
- 1 1/2- 2 cups of micro or field salad greens
- 1 Fiji apple, cored and sliced
- 1 shallot, minced
- 1/2 cup of walnuts
- 8 Mission figs, cut into quarters

Ingredients for Dressing
- 1/4 cup of walnut oil
- 1 teaspoon of ground mustard powder
- 1/2 cup of white wine vinegar
- 1 Mission fig
- Salt and pepper to taste

1. In a bowl, mix the greens, apples, shallot, walnuts, and figs.
2. In a blender, add walnut oil, mustard powder, white, wine, vinegar, fig, salt and pepper.
3. Blend for 30 seconds, until the fig is creamy.
4. Pour dressing over salad. Serve.

Prep time: 8 minutes

Nutrients per serving: Calories: 157, Total Fat: 16 g, Sat. Fat: 1 g, Carbs: 21 g, Fiber: 4 g, Sugars: 16 g, Protein: 3 g, Sodium: 5 mg, Cholesterol: 0 mg

"If you don't take care of your body,
where are you going to live?"
~Unknown

Strawberry Spinach Crunch

I had this salad in a restaurant and fell in love with the sweet, crunchy, pungent combination of strawberries, walnuts and onions. This salad has loads of Vitamin C and more fiber than orange juice. Vitamin C is essential to maintaining strong blood vessels for heart health and beautiful skin to age gracefully.
Makes 4 servings.

Ingredients for Dressing
1/4 cup of safflower oil
1 tablespoon of red wine vinegar
1 teaspoon of agave
1/4 teaspoon of ground ginger

Ingredients for Salad
1 cup of fresh strawberries, chopped
2 cups of spinach, rinsed and dried
1/2 cup of walnuts, chopped
1/2 cup of red onions, finely chopped

1. In a small bowl, whisk oil, vinegar, agave, and ginger until well mixed into a dressing.
2. Put field greens in a big bowl; top with strawberries, walnuts and red onions.
3. Pour dressing over mixture and toss to combine.

Prep time: 9 minutes

Nutrients per serving: Calories: 255, Total Fat: 23 g, Sat. Fat: 1 g, Carbs: 10 g, Fiber: 3 g, Sugars: 5 g, Protein: 5 g, Sodium: 39 mg, Cholesterol: 0 mg

"From the bitterness of disease man learns the sweetness of health."
~Catalan Proverb

Oh My Darling Clementine Salad

This salad is a favorite of adults and children. It's a great example of how a salad can be simple yet filled with powerful nutrients and antioxidants at the same time. Adding this to your meal gives you these benefits with just two ingredients. The cinnamon has a bright flavor and gives an added blood sugar balancing component to balance the fruit.
Makes 8 servings.

Dressing ingredients:

2 tablespoons of extra virgin olive oil

2 tablespoons of clementine juice (approximately 1 clementine)

1/8 teaspoon of sea salt

1/8 teaspoon of pepper

1/8 teaspoon of coriander

1/8 teaspoon of cinnamon

1/8 teaspoon of maple syrup

Salad ingredients

6 - 8 cups of baby spinach leaves

6 clementines, peeled and segmented

1. Whisk the oil, juice, salt, pepper, coriander, cinnamon, and syrup together.
2. In a bowl add the spinach leaves and clementines
3. Pour salad dressing over the salad and toss.

Prep time: 10 minutes

Nutrients per serving: Calories: 41, Total Fat: 0 g, Sat. Fat: 0 g, Carbs: 10 g, Fiber: 1 g, Sugars: 6 g, Protein: 1 g, Sodium: 74 mg, Cholesterol: 0 mg

"If you truly get in touch with a piece of carrot, you get in touch with the soil, the rain, the sunshine. You get in touch with Mother Earth and eating in such a way, you feel in touch with true life, your roots, and that is meditation. If we chew every morsel of our food in that way we become grateful and when you are grateful, you are happy."
Thich Nhat Hanh

Surprise! It's Kale in A Salad

This is a new twist on kale because it is not cooked. The acids from the lemon and orange juices actually soften and sweeten the kale. Kale has antioxidant and anti-inflammatory roles that reverse chronic inflammation down to the genes. Chronic inflammation increases the risk of heart disease, diabetes and high blood pressure, high cholesterol and obesity. It is important to eat foods that reverse that process several times per week. Makes 8 servings.

1 bunch of fresh kale

3/4 cup of extra virgin olive oil

1/2 cup of lemon juice

1/2 cup of orange juice

1 teaspoon of sea salt

1 medium tomato, diced (optional)

1/2 cup of carrots, grated

1/4 cup of mushrooms, thinly sliced

1/2 chopped avocado

1/8 teaspoon of cayenne pepper

1 clove garlic, crushed

1/2 teaspoon of oregano

1/2 teaspoon of thyme

1/2 teaspoon of rosemary

1. Wash the kale leaves and tear them into bite-sized pieces, removing the tough stems.
2. Add the olive oil, lemon juice, orange juice and salt. Stir well to make sure you tenderize the leaves.
3. Let rest for 30 minutes.
4. Add tomatoes, carrots, mushroom, cayenne pepper, garlic, avocado, oregano, thyme, and rosemary.
5. Toss to mix herbs and the salad.

Prep time: 12 minutes
Marinade time: 30 minutes

Nutrients per serving: Calories: 254, Total Fat: 24 g, Sat. Fat: 3 g, Carbs: 11 g, Fiber: 3 g, Sugars: 2 g, Protein: 2 g, Sodium: 80 mg, Cholesterol: 0 mg

Tomato-Basil Chickpea Salad

Tomato-Basil Chickpea Salad is flexible, so you can use it in a variety of ways. Tomatoes and chickpeas have been shown to help lower cholesterol and lower triglycerides. Chickpeas also have a positive effect on modulating appetite. They've also been shown to support insulin release, so they balance blood sugars and help with weight loss in addition to lowering cholesterol.
Makes 6 servings.

Dressing ingredients:

1/4 cup of extra virgin olive oil

2 tablespoons of white wine vinegar

1 teaspoon of sea salt

1/2 teaspoon of freshly ground pepper

Salad ingredients:

1 cup of cooked chickpeas (may use canned)

3 plum tomatoes (or freshest variety available), chopped

1 cup of red onion, chopped

1 cup of fresh basil, chopped

1. In a small bowl, combine olive oil, vinegar, salt and pepper.
2. In a large bowl, combine the chickpeas, tomatoes and onion.
3. Pour salad dressing over mixture and toss.
4. Top with fresh basil.

Prep time: 10 minutes

Nutrients per serving: Calories: 156, Total Fat: 10 g, Sat. Fat: 1 g, Carbs: 14 g, Fiber: 3 g, Sugars: 2 g, Protein: 4 g, Sodium: 140 mg, Cholesterol: 0 mg

"Cooking with your kids and engaging them in hands-on activities are two ways to begin to educate children about the healthy eating, and kick start the important task to help change how the younger generation looks at food and nutrition."
Marcus Samuelsson

Minty Lentil Salad

In this recipe you simply boil the lentils and let the mint in the salad dressing punch up the flavor in the salad. Lentils are a great source of plant-based protein and soluble fiber. Perfect for reducing digestive issues, high cholesterol levels and heart disease. The fiber also helps with diabetes and satiety for weight loss. Makes 6 servings.

Dressing ingredients:

1/4 cup of extra virgin olive oil

1/4 cup of red wine vinegar

4 cloves garlic, minced

1/2 teaspoon of ground cumin

1/2 teaspoon of sea salt

1/2 teaspoon of pepper

Salad ingredients:

3 cups of water

1 cup of green lentils

1 cup of finely chopped red onion

1 red, yellow or orange bell pepper, diced

1/4 cup of chopped fresh mint

1. In a small bowl, whisk together olive oil, vinegar, garlic, cumin, salt and pepper.
2. In a saucepan, add 3 cups of water and bring to a boil.
3. Rinse the lentils and drain. Add them to the water and reduce heat. Simmer uncovered for 15-20 minutes.
4. Once they are tender, drain and place in a bowl.
5. Add bell pepper and red onions. Gently pour the salad dressing over the lentil mixture.
6. Top with chopped mint.

Prep time: 10 minutes
Cook time: 20 minutes

Nutrients per serving: Calories: 259, Total Fat: 10 g, Sat. Fat: 1 g, Carbs: 31 g, Fiber: 12 g, Sugars: 4 g, Protein: 13 g, Sodium: 201 mg, Cholesterol: 0 mg

"There is no sincerer love than the love of food."
George Bernard Shaw

52

Mango Orange Salad

The sweetness of the tropical fruit in this salad makes it a favorite of children. Mangoes and oranges both have antioxidants that have been shown to reduce the risk of certain cancers. The antioxidants are preventative of cancer and damage to cells due to stress. Makes 6 servings.

Dressing Ingredients
Juice of 2 limes, squeezed
Juice of 1 orange, squeezed
1/8 cup of fresh cilantro, chopped
1/4 cup of extra virgin olive oil
1 teaspoon of agave

1 teaspoon of grated ginger
Sea salt to taste
Salad Ingredients
2 mangoes diced
2 oranges sliced
1/4 cup of scallions sliced
4 cups of field greens, washed

1. In a shaker container, add lime juice, orange juice, cilantro, oil, agave, ginger and sea salt.
2. Shake well.
1. In a large bowl, place the field greens.
3. Add mangoes, oranges and scallions.
4. Pour dressing over the salad and toss.

Prep time: 10 minutes

Nutrients per serving: Calories: 139, Total Fat: 10 g, Sat. Fat: 1 g, Carbs: 14 g, Fiber: 2 g, Sugars: 10 g, Protein: 1 g, Sodium: 9 mg, Cholesterol: 0 mg

"Salad can get a bad rap. People think of bland and watery iceberg lettuce, but in fact, salads are an art form, from the simplest rendition to a colorful kitchen-sink approach."
Marcus Samuelsson

Couscous Olive Salad

Olives are pure salty goodness that certainly satisfies our need for salt. Olives are perfect for anyone who is following an anti-inflammatory diet. They are a source of healthy fat and fiber. They have also been shown to help with allergies by reducing the histamine response. You can say bye-bye to anti-histamines if you say hello to olives. Makes 6 servings.

Dressing Ingredients

1/4 cup extra virgin olive oil

2 tablespoons of balsamic vinegar

1/4 teaspoon of maple syrup

Pinch of sea salt

1 tablespoon of parsley, chopped

Salad Ingredients

2 cups of arugula

1 cup of cucumber, sliced

1 cup of couscous, cooked

1 cup of grape tomatoes, whole

3/4 cup of Kalamata olives

1. In a shaker container, add oil, vinegar, maple syrup sea salt and parsley.
2. Shake well.
3. Place the arugula in a large bowl.
4. Add cucumbers, couscous, tomatoes and olives.
5. Toss with salad dressing and serve.

Prep time: 10 minutes

Nutrients per serving: Calories: 158, Total Fat: 14 g, Sat. Fat: 2 g, Carbs: 7 g, Fiber: 1 g, Sugars: 1 g, Protein: 1 g, Sodium: 36 mg, Cholesterol: 0 mg

"Salad can get a bad rap. People think of bland and watery iceberg lettuce, but in fact, salads are an art form, from the simplest rendition to a colorful kitchen-sink approach."
Marcus Samuelsson

Rice Noodle Salad with Lime Peanut Dressing

This salad originally started out as a mason jar salad that I took in my lunch box. It was so good that I shared it with friends at lunch. Red cabbage is a member of the cruciferous vegetable family so it has anti-inflammatory and anti-cancer properties. The red purplish color is anti-aging and stress reducing as well. Makes 8 servings.

Dressing ingredients:

2 tablespoons of toasted sesame oil

6 tablespoons of water

1 teaspoon of natural peanut butter

1 teaspoon of lime juice

1 teaspoon of Braggs Liquid amino acids

1/4 teaspoon of maple syrup

Salad ingredients:

1 cup of cucumber, sliced

1 cup of red, yellow and orange bell peppers, sliced

1 cup of carrots, shredded

1 cup of rice noodles, cooked

2 teaspoons of cilantro, finely chopped

1 scallion, chopped

1/2 cup of peanuts, chopped

2 cup of red cabbage, sliced

1 tablespoon of sesame seeds

1. Grate the carrot and cabbage together in a large bowl.
2. Add bell peppers, rice noodles, cilantro, scallions, and peanuts to the bowl.
3. In a separate small bowl, whisk together sesame oil, water, peanut butter, lime juice, Braggs and maple syrup.
4. Pour dressing over salad and toss. Serve.

Prep time: 10 minutes

Nutrients per serving: Calories: 149, Total Fat: 10 g, Sat. Fat: 1 g, Carbs: 12 g, Fiber: 3 g, Sugars: 3 g, Protein: 4 g, Sodium: 65 mg, Cholesterol: 0 mg

"Eating is a natural way to feel happy. Overeating isn't." – Deepak Chopra From his new book what are you hungry for?

 # NOTES

Exciting Entrees

Vegetable Pasta with Pesto

I started out making this recipe with pasta and vegetables then I decided to skip the pasta all together.
By replacing the pasta with vegetables, the servings of fiber are increased in this dish. High fiber meals are beneficial to heart health and digestive support.
Mushrooms support the immune system by reducing inflammation. Crimini mushrooms, in particular, are a valuable source of vitamin B12. This is great news for vegans.
Makes 4 servings.

Almond pesto

Juice of one lemon

2 cups of tightly packed, fresh Basil leaves

1 cup of almonds

1 small garlic clove

2 tablespoons of extra virgin olive oil

1/2 teaspoon of sea salt

Vegetable Pasta

2 yellow squash

1 cup of mushrooms, diced

1 orange bell pepper, diced

1. In a blender, add lemon juice, basil, garlic, almonds, extra virgin olive oil and sea salt; blend until it becomes a thick paste. Reserve 1 teaspoon of extra virgin olive oil for sautéing.
2. Cut the yellow squash into long strips or use a spiralizer.
3. In a saucepan, add olive oil, mushrooms and orange bell peppers; sauté until tender.
4. Add pesto and toss them together.

Nutrients per serving: Calories: 230, Total Fat: 19 g, Sat. Fat: 2 g, Carbs: 12 g, Fiber: 5 g, Sugars: 4 g, Protein: 7 g, Sodium: 127 mg, Cholesterol: 0 mg

"Food is your body's fuel. Without fuel, your body wants to shut down."
Ken Hill

Bok Choy Stir-Fry

I love a good one-pot meal and this one of them. Bok choy is part of the cruciferous vegetable family, so it has antioxidant properties that destroy free radicals and protect cells from damage. Antioxidants are cancer preventative as well.
Makes 6 servings.

2 teaspoons extra of virgin olive oil

1 small yellow onion, diced

3 garlic cloves, crushed

1 inch of ginger root, peeled and grated, or 1/2 teaspoon ginger powder

1 carrot, thinly sliced

2 cups of cooked chickpeas (may use canned)

2 cups of baby bok choy, washed and chopped

1 teaspoon of sesame oil

1. In a saucepan on medium heat, add olive oil, onion, garlic and ginger; sauté for 2 minutes.
2. Add the carrots, bok choy and chickpeas; cook for another 5 minutes.
3. Drizzle with sesame oil and serve.

Prep time: 10 minutes
Cook time: 7 minutes

Nutrients per serving: Calories: 158, Total Fat: 6 g, Sat. Fat: 1 g, Carbs: 21 g, Fiber: 4 g, Sugars: 1 g, Protein: 5 g, Sodium: 262 mg, Cholesterol: 0 mg

"Every time you use the word 'healthy,' you lose. The key is to make yummy, delicious food that happens to be healthy."
Marcus Samuelsson

Mediterranean Stuffed Zucchini

*Don't be afraid to stuff your vegetables with vegetables.
The results can be amazing! Zucchini contains folate, B6, B1,
B2, B3, choline, zinc, magnesium, and omega-3 fatty acids.
Zucchini's abundance of nutrients is essential for blood sugar
regulation. Makes 4 servings.*

4 zucchini or summer squash

1/8 cup of extra virgin olive oil

2 teaspoons of sea salt

1/2 cup of red onions, chopped

5-6 garlic cloves, chopped

2 cups of spinach, chopped

1/2 teaspoon of cumin

1 teaspoon of coriander

1/2 teaspoon of pepper

Ingredients for dressing

1/8 cup of extra virgin olive oil

Juice of 2 limes

1 teaspoon of coriander

1/2 teaspoon of sea salt

1. Preheat the oven to 375 °F.
2. Split the zucchini in half and scoop out the middle.
3. Place the scooped out squash onto the cutting board.
4. Drizzle oil on the zucchini halves that have been scooped out (reserve 1/8 cup of oil for the salad dressing) and sea salt (reserve 1/2 teaspoons of salt for later).
5. Place on a cookie sheet and bake for 10- 12 minutes.

Stuffing
1. Chop the zucchini middle into small pieces and put them in the sauté pan.
2. Add 1 teaspoon of oil, onions, garlic, spinach, cumin, coriander, salt and pepper.
3. Sauté for 4 minutes.
4. Once the zucchini is done, drizzle the dressing on the inside of the zucchini.
5. Fill with the stuffing and drizzle more dressing on top of the stuffing.
6. Serve over green lentils and quinoa with dressing (lentil quinoa salad).

Prep time: 5 minutes
Cook time: 4 minutes
Bake time: 12 minutes

Nutrients per serving: Calories: 186, Total Fat: 15 g, Sat. Fat: 2 g, Carbs: 14 g, Fiber: 4 g, Sugars: 5 g, Protein: 4 g, Sodium: 176 mg, Cholesterol: 0 mg

Lentil Quinoa Salad

This salad can be used as a main dish or a side dish. Lentils are a great source of protein and soluble fiber. They promote the lowering of cholesterol levels and helps with satiety at the same time. Quinoa is packed with protein and it has many anti-inflammatory phytonutrients as well. This dish is a home-run for anyone with heart problems including high blood pressure and high cholesterol. Makes 6 servings.

Salad Ingredients

1 cup of dry green lentils
4 cups of water
1 cup of vegetable broth
1 cup of quinoa or couscous

Dressing Ingredients

1/2 cup of extra virgin olive oil
1 teaspoon of coriander
Juice of 2 limes, squeezed
1/2 teaspoon of salt

1. Bring the water to a boil.
2. While the water is coming to a boil, rinse the lentils well.
3. Add the lentils to the water; cook for 20 minutes or until done.
4. Bring the vegetable broth to a boil.
5. While the water is coming to a boil, rinse the quinoa well.
6. Add the quinoa to the broth; cook for 20 minutes until done.
7. Fluff quinoa with a fork.
8. In a small bowl combine the oil, coriander, lime and salt. Gently whisk.
9. On a platter mix the lentils and quinoa and generously drizzle the dressing.

Prep time: 5 minutes
Cook time: 40 minutes

Nutrients per serving: Calories: 344, Total Fat: 12 g, Sat. Fat: 2 g, Carbs: 46 g, Fiber: 13 g, Sugars: 3 g, Protein: 16 g, Sodium: 83 mg, Cholesterol: 0 mg

Sweet Potato Stir-Fry

Sweet potatoes have been touted as a super food for good reason! Sweet potatoes are high in antioxidants, anti-inflammatory, and blood sugar-regulating nutrients. These properties make sweet potatoes an excellent option for people living with chronic disease such as diabetes, obesity, heart disease, high cholesterol, or hypertension.
Note: Traditional Worchester sauce contains animal products, like oyster sauce so make sure you look for the vegetarian version. Makes 6 servings.

3 teaspoons of extra virgin olive oil

1 small sweet potato, diced

3 garlic cloves, chopped

1 small onion, chopped

1 teaspoon of fresh ginger, minced or grated

1/2 cup of zucchini, chopped

1/2 cup of celery, chopped

1 cup of baby bok choy, chopped

1 1/2 cup of black beans, cooked (or one 15 ounce can)

2 teaspoons of tamari or soy sauce

1 teaspoon of vegan Worchester sauce

1. In a large sauce pan, add oil, sweet potato, garlic, onion and ginger; sauté for 12 minutes.
2. Add zucchini, celery, bok choy and black beans; cook for another 7 minutes or until sweet potatoes are soft.
3. Remove from the heat and stir in tamari and Worchester sauce.

Prep time: 14 minutes
Cook time: 20 minutes

Nutrients per serving: Calories: 94, Total Fat: 1 g, Sat. Fat: 0 g, Carbs: 17 g, Fiber: 6 g, Sugars: 2 g, Protein: 5 g, Sodium: 300 mg, Cholesterol: 0 mg

"Fill your plate with the colors of the rainbow What pleases the eye pleases the body as a whole" - Deepak Chopra From his new book What are you hungry for?

Veggies coated with Pesto

This recipe goes well with Nutty Rice with Mushrooms, or another whole grain dish. The combination of vegetables in this dish has antioxidant, anti-inflammatory and anti-cancer properties. They also aid in balancing blood sugar. Take your pick of which chronic illness this recipe helps to do away with.
Makes 6 servings.

Pesto Ingredients:
1 cup of fresh basil leaves
1 tablespoon of pine nuts
3 tablespoons of extra virgin olive oil
1 tablespoon of water
1 garlic clove
1/4 cup of cooked white beans (may use canned)
1/4 teaspoon of sea salt

Veggie Ingredients:
2 tablespoons of extra virgin olive oil
1/4 teaspoon of black pepper
1/4 teaspoon of sea salt
1 carrot, peeled and cut into strips
1 medium zucchini, sliced
1 cup of eggplant, sliced
1/2 cup of red onion, sliced
1/2 cup of bell pepper, sliced

1. Pesto: Place basil, pine nuts, oil, water, garlic, white beans, salt and pepper in a blender; blend for 45 seconds or until creamy.
2. In a saucepan over medium heat, add olive oil, salt and pepper; add carrots, zucchini, eggplant, onion and bell peppers.
3. Sauté for 5-8 minutes.
4. Remove from heat and toss with pesto.
5. Serve warm or room temperature.

Prep time: 13 minutes
Cook time: 8 minutes

Nutrients per serving: Calories: 103, Total Fat: 8 g, Sat. Fat: 1 g, Carbs: 8 g, Fiber: 3 g, Sugars: 3 g, Protein: 2 g, Sodium: 191 mg, Cholesterol: 0 mg

Spicy Cashew Green Beans

Green beans are high in vitamin C, beta-carotene, and manganese. It has other antioxidants that support heart health and cell repair. Cashews are high in antioxidants too. This is a supercharged antioxidant and anti-aging dish. Makes 4 servings.

1/2 pound of green beans, washed and trimmed

2 tablespoons of extra virgin olive oil

1/2 cup of red onion, chopped

1/2 cup of raw cashews

Pinch of sea salt to taste

Pinch of black pepper

1 teaspoon of paprika

1 teaspoon of fresh flat leaf parsley, chopped

1. In a 4-quart pan, heat water to a boil; cook the green beans for 3-4 minutes. Drain in a colander and run cold water over the green beans immediately to stop the cooking process.
2. In a frying pan, add olive oil, onions, cashews, salt, pepper and paprika. Cook for 2 minutes on medium heat.
3. Add the green beans and cook for another 4 minutes.
4. Sprinkle parsley on top and serve.

Prep time: 10 minutes
Cook time: 15 minutes

Nutrients per serving: Calories: 196, Total Fat: 15 g, Sat. Fat: 3 g, Carbs: 14 g, Fiber: 4 g, Sugars: 3 g, Protein: 4 g, Sodium: 35 mg, Cholesterol: 0 mg

"Not everyone can afford to eat well in America, which is a literal shame, but most of us can: Americans spend less than 10 percent of their income on food, less than the citizens of any other nation. "
Michael Pollan, Food Rules: An Eater's Manual

Sunchoke Stir-fry

These root vegetables have soluble fiber and can be eaten raw or cooked. Sunchokes have a substance called inulin that supports the growth of healthy probiotics in the digestive tract. Probiotics are essential for immune function and healthy digestion.
Note: Traditional Worchester sauce contains animal products, like oyster sauce so make sure you look for the vegetarian version. Makes 6 servings.

1 tablespoon of olive oil
1 cup of red onions, chopped
4 garlic cloves, crushed
1 cup of sunchokes
1 1/2 tablespoon of grated ginger
1 cup of mushrooms, chopped
2 cups of bok choy, chopped
1 cup of white beans

2 tablespoons of Worchester sauce (look for vegan version)
1 tablespoon of tamari or soy sauce
2 tablespoons of sesame seeds
1 tablespoon of toasted sesame oil
2 cups of brown rice

1. In a large sauce pan, add oil, onions, garlic, sunchokes, ginger, and mushrooms.
2. Sauté on medium heat for 6 minutes or until the onions are translucent.
3. Stir in bok choy, white beans, Worchester sauce, tamari, and sesame seeds. Sauté for 2 more minutes.
4. Drizzle with sesame oil once the stir-fry is taken off the heat.
5. Serve over rice.

Prep time: 10 minutes
Cook time: 10 minutes

Nutrients per serving: Calories: 213, Total Fat: 9 g, Sat. Fat: 1 g, Carbs: 28 g, Fiber: 6 g, Sugars: 2 g, Protein: 3 g, Sodium: 198 mg, Cholesterol: 0 mg

Bella Burgers

Everyone loves burgers. They are filling and awesome on the grill! Using a portabella mushroom as the burger is a twist that supports your immune system in overcoming colds, flu, allergies and so much more. For those suffering from auto-immune diseases mushrooms support the immune response without over stimulating it. The high fiber content helps control blood sugar and cholesterol levels. This burger is great for your health. Makes 4 servings.

6 garlic cloves

2 tablespoons of balsamic vinegar

1/4 cup of fresh chives, chopped

1/8 teaspoon of black pepper

4 medium Portobello mushrooms

1/2 cup of red onions, sliced

1/4 cup of extra virgin olive oil

1/2 cup of lettuce, chopped

1/2 cup of sliced tomatoes (optional)

4 teaspoons of Dijon mustard

4 whole grain buns or gluten free bread or whole wheat tortillas

1. In a medium bowl, add garlic, balsamic vinegar, chives, and pepper. Marinate the mushrooms in this mixture for at least 1 hour.

2. In a saucepan, add the red onions and olive oil; sauté for 2 minutes.

3. Add Portobello mushrooms; cook until soft, about 5-8 minutes.

4. Serve on a whole grain bun with sliced tomatoes, lettuce and mustard.

Prep time: 15 minutes
Marinade time: up to 1 hour
Cook time: 8 minutes

Nutrients per serving: Calories: 252, Total Fat: 10 g, Sat. Fat: 2 g, Carbs: 33 g, Fiber: 6 g, Sugars: 7 g, Protein: 10 g, Sodium: 285 mg, Cholesterol: 0 mg

Curry Sweet Potatoes

If sweet potatoes are considered a "superfood" then curry should be considered a "super spice". Curry is actually a combination of spices that includes turmeric.
Turmeric is an anti-inflammatory, so it protects cells from damage and premature cell death. When you combine turmeric with sweet potatoes, you create an anti-inflammatory dish that is not only delicious, but it also aids in the healing chronic of conditions including cancer, diabetes and heart disease.
Makes 6 servings.

1 tablespoon of olive oil
1/2 cup of yellow onions, chopped
1/2 teaspoon sea salt
1 tablespoon of curry powder
1/2 teaspoon of cumin

1/2 teaspoon of ginger
1/4 teaspoon of cinnamon
3 small sweet potatoes, cubed
1/2 cup of coconut milk
3 cups of spinach
4 cups of cooked quinoa

1. In a soup pot, add oil, onion, salt, curry powder, cumin, ginger, cinnamon, sweet potatoes, and coconut milk.
2. Sauté on medium heat for 12-15 minutes.
3. Stir in spinach; simmer for another 2-3 minutes.
4. Serve over quinoa.

Prep time: 10 minutes
Cook time: 18 minutes

Nutrients per serving: Calories: 128, Total Fat: 7 g, Sat. Fat: 4 g, Carbs: 16 g, Fiber: 3 g, Sugars: 3 g, Protein: 2 g, Sodium: 154 mg, Cholesterol: 0 mg

Eggplant Lasagna

Who doesn't love lasagna? The great thing about this recipe is that the eggplant serves as the lasagna noodles. Tomatoes, beans, and almonds all have soluble fiber which has been shown to help lower cholesterol and triglycerides. The fiber can also balance blood sugar levels. Makes 6 servings.

3/4 cup of raw almonds

2 tablespoons of Italian seasoning

1/2 teaspoon of black pepper

1/2 teaspoon of sea salt

1 cup of water

1 large eggplant, sliced into 1/8-inch disks

2 tablespoons of extra virgin olive oil

1 cup of yellow onion, diced

4 cups of fresh spinach, chopped

1 1/2 cup of cooked cannellini beans (15 ounce can, drained)

1 cup of tomato basil sauce or your favorite tomato sauce

*1 cup Daiya Mozzarella Style, Shredded Vegan Cheese

1. Place almonds in a blender and grind to a fine powder.
2. Mix almond crumbs, Italian seasoning, pepper and salt.
3. Dip eggplant slices into water.
4. Thoroughly coat each slice in almond crumbs.
5. In a saucepan, heat the oil and gently sauté the eggplant for 2 minutes on each side or until tender. Remove from the heat and place on paper towels to remove excess oil. Complete all the pieces of eggplant.
6. Preheat the oven to 350°.
7. In a saucepan over medium heat add oil, onions and spinach. Sauté for 5 minutes.
8. In the bottom of a casserole pan, layer the eggplant to cover the bottom. Then, pour the spinach mixture over the eggplant slices.
9. Add the tomato sauce and grated vegan cheese. Bake for 20 minutes.

Prep time: 10 minutes
Cook time: 15 minutes
Bake time: 20 minutes

Nutrients per serving: Calories: 214, Total Fat: 11 g, Sat. Fat: 1 g, Carbs: 24 g, Fiber: 8 g, Sugars: 5 g, Protein: 9 g, Sodium: 134 mg, Cholesterol: 0 mg

Eggplant Envelopes

An Italian friend introduced me to eggplant and it was love at first taste. The roasted red bell pepper in this recipe deepens the flavor of the eggplant while protecting your cells. The tomato sauce adds lycopene and fiber to this lunch special without the fat from mayonnaise found in most sandwiches.
Makes 8 servings.

1 baby eggplant
1 teaspoon of sea salt
1 tablespoon of black pepper
2 tablespoons of Italian seasoning
1 tablespoon of extra virgin olive oil
2 garlic cloves, minced

4 whole wheat tortillas or gluten-free tortilla
1 cup of tomato sauce (Tomato Basil or your favorite)
1 cup of roasted red pepper, sliced (optional)
2 cups of romaine lettuce, chopped

1. Cut off the ends of the eggplant, and thinly slice lengthwise (approximately 1/8 inch). Season the eggplant with salt, pepper and Italian seasoning.
2. In a saucepan, add olive oil and garlic; cook on medium-low heat for 1 minute.
3. Add eggplant to the pan; sauté for approximately 4 minutes or until soft (translucent).
4. Warm the tortilla in the oven for 1 minute.
5. Place the tortilla on a plate and spread with 1 tablespoon of tomato sauce.
6. Place a couple of roasted red pepper slices and 1/4 cup of romaine lettuce on the tortilla.
7. Finally, add 3-4 slices of eggplant on top of the lettuce.
8. Roll the tortilla away from you until it looks like a burrito. Repeat for all tortillas, and serve.

Prep time: 15 minutes
Cook time: 10 minutes

Nutrients per serving: Calories: 112, Total Fat: 4 g, Sat. Fat: 0 g, Carbs: 18 g, Fiber: 2 g, Sugars: 1 g, Protein: 3 g, Sodium: 222 mg, Cholesterol: 0 mg

Hummus Half-Moon Pies

You can hide vegetables inside the tortillas!
The main ingredient in hummus is chickpeas. Chickpeas have been shown to support insulin release, so they balance blood sugars and help with weight loss in addition to lowering cholesterol. Recent research has found that people who supplemented their diets with chickpeas consumed fewer snacks and fewer overall calories. Makes 6 servings.

4-6 whole wheat tortillas

1 cup of hummus or roasted red pepper hummus in this book

1/2 cup of scallions, chopped

1/2 cup of salsa

1/2 cup of mushrooms, minced

1/2 cup of carrots, grated

1. Take one tortilla and add about 1 tablespoon of hummus, spread evenly.
2. Add a teaspoon each of scallions, salsa, mushrooms and carrots and fold in half creating a half moon.
3. On medium heat (with no oil in the pan) place the half-moon on the pan to warm for 30-45 seconds. Turn it over and heat for another 30 seconds.

Prep time: 10 minutes

Nutrients per serving: Calories: 229, Total Fat: 7 g, Sat. Fat: 1 g, Carbs: 36 g, Fiber: 2 g, Sugars: 1 g, Protein: 7 g, Sodium: 276 mg, Cholesterol: 0 mg

Just like keeping a healthy diet is important to maintaining a healthy lifestyle, eating the right foods is just as important for getting the most out of your workout.
Marcus Samuelsson

Nut Loaf

There is something quite comforting about rich, filling slices of meatloaf and you will have the same feeling from this dish. The four different types of nuts provide healthy oils and proteins that stick to your ribs like meatloaf, but vegan style. The mushrooms add immune boosting support. Makes 8 servings.

2 tablespoons of extra virgin olive oil

1 cup of chopped yellow onion

4 garlic cloves, chopped

2 small Portobello mushrooms, chopped

1 cup of vegetable stock (check label to make sure gluten-free)

2 teaspoons of arrowroot (or corn starch or flour)

1 cup of raw cashews

1 cup of raw pecans

1 cup of raw Brazil nuts

1 cup of raw almonds

2 teaspoons of chopped hot or sweet pepper

2 teaspoons of white wine vinegar

2 teaspoons of dried oregano

1/2 teaspoon of sea salt

1 teaspoon of black pepper

1. Preheat the oven to 375°F. Oil a loaf pan.
2. In a saucepan over medium heat, add the olive oil, garlic, onions and mushrooms. Cook for 5 minutes, stirring occasionally.
3. Add the vegetable broth and arrowroot powder, stirring until it begins to thicken--about 5-8 minutes. Remove from heat.
4. In a food processor or blender, add the cashews, pecans, Brazil nuts, almonds, pepper, vinegar, oregano, salt and pepper. Blend until coarse--about 30 seconds.
5. Combine with ingredients from the saucepan into the food processor and blend for 30 seconds.
6. Pour mixture into the loaf pan and bake for 30-40 minutes.

Prep time: 5 minutes
Cook time: 10 minutes
Bake time: 40 minutes

Nutrients per serving: Calories: 523, Total Fat: 42 g, Sat. Fat: 5 g, Carbs: 32 g, Fiber: 6 g, Sugars: 5 g, Protein: 13 g, Sodium: 134 mg, Cholesterol: 0 mg

Vegetarian Lettuce Wraps

The lettuce serves as the taco, so it's fun and filling at the same time. This wrap is a perfectly balanced meal with a combination of healthy fat, carbohydrates and protein. These ingredients will stabilize blood sugars for diabetes and pre diabetes. The vegetable toppings have antioxidant properties that support cell repair. They also have heart health, anti-cancer and anti-aging benefits. Makes 8 servings.

1/2 package of bean thread noodles**

1/4 cup of natural peanut butter

2 tablespoons of tamari

1/4 cup of agave

Juice of 1 lime

1 teaspoon of chili powder

1 teaspoon of sesame oil

1 teaspoon of olive oil

1/2 cup of red onions, minced

1/2 cup of carrot, shredded

1/2 cup of celery, chopped

1 cup bok choy or your favorite cabbage, chopped

1/2 cup of peanuts (or any roasted nuts), chopped

1 head lettuce separated and washed (Romaine, Boston, etc.)

1/2 cup of fresh cilantro, chopped

1/4 cup of scallions, chopped

1 lime, sliced into wedges

** You can substitute thin rice noodles for the bean thread noodles

1. Cook the noodles according to package directions. While the noodles are cooking, make dressing in a small bowl by combining peanut butter, tamari, agave, lime, chili powder, and sesame oil.
2. Heat olive oil in a saucepan over medium-low heat. Add onions, carrots, celery, and bok choy. Cook for 4 minutes.
3. Add noodles and peanuts; mix well. Remove from heat.
4. Add dressing to the mixture.
5. Take a lettuce leaf and add a spoonful of filling. Top with scallions and cilantro.
6. Squeeze lime juice over filling and serve.

Prep time: 12 minutes
Cook time: 5 minutes

Nutrients per serving: Calories: 238, Total Fat: 10 g, Sat. Fat: 2 g, Carbs: 32 g, Fiber: 5 g, Sugars: 5 g, Protein: 9 g, Sodium: 332 mg, Cholesterol: 0 mg

Veggie Ciabatta Sandwich

This sandwich was developed using leftovers from the night before. Summer squash and zucchini contain nutrients essential for healthy blood sugar levels and satiety. If you want to add vegan cheese, go for it and enjoy the texture.
Makes 2 Sandwiches.

2 Ciabatta rolls
1 teaspoon of extra virgin olive oil
1/2 cup of yellow onion
1/4 teaspoon of sea salt
1/4 teaspoon of pepper
2 cloves of garlic, minced
1/2 cup of zucchini, diced

1/2 cup of summer squash, diced
1 cup of spinach, chopped
*1/8 teaspoon of hot peppers, minced
* Add vegan cheese
*optional

1. Toast the bread before putting the veggies on it.
2. In a sauce pan over medium-low heat, add onion, sea salt, garlic and pepper; sauté for 2 minutes.
3. Add the zucchini and squash; sauté for another 3 minutes.
4. Add spinach; sauté for another minute. Turn off the heat.
5. Spoon the sautéed vegetables on to the toasted bread.
6. Cover with 1 slice of cheese creating an open-faced sandwich.
7. Put the sandwich under the broiler for one minute to melt the cheese and enjoy it.

Prep time: 5 minutes
Cook time: 10 minutes

Nutrients per serving: Calories: 311, Total Fat: 7 g, Sat. Fat: 1 g, Carbs: 55 g, Fiber: 7 g, Sugars: 6 g, Protein: 10 g, Sodium: 125 mg, Cholesterol: 0 mg

Vegetable Enchiladas

I fell in love with enchiladas long ago because you can stuff them with so many different fillings. This version has Swiss chard, black beans and corn. Swiss chard and tomato sauce have antioxidants and anti-inflammatory properties. The nutrients in them have been shown to protect from bone loss. Black beans and corn kernels balance blood sugar. Makes 6 servings.

1 bunch of Swiss chard

2 teaspoons of extra virgin olive oil

6 garlic cloves, minced

1/2 cup of red onion, chopped

1 1/2 teaspoon of cumin

1/2 teaspoon of cayenne

1 teaspoon of sea salt

1 1/2 cups of black beans (15 ounce can, drained)

1 cup of corn kernels, fresh or frozen

Juice of 1 lime

8 corn tortillas

2 cups of Spicy Tomato sauce (see recipe in the Vital Vegetables sections)

1. De-vein the Swiss chard by pulling the leaves from the stem. Place them in a large bowl filled with cold water. This will wash dirt from the leaves and help them wilt during cooking.

2. Chop the leaves into small pieces that will fit into the enchilada.

3. In a sauté pan on medium-low heat, add oil, garlic, red onions, cumin, cayenne, and sea salt; sauté for 1 minute.

4. Add the Swiss chard; cook for another 2 minutes, turning the chard until it wilts.

5. Add black beans and corn; sauté for another 2 minutes. Turn off heat.

6. In a small sauce pan, add 1/4 teaspoon of olive oil and lightly cook each tortilla on both sides.

7. In a baking dish, take a corn tortilla; add 2-3 tablespoons of the Swiss chard filling on the 1/3 of tortilla; roll into a cigar-like shape.

8. Repeat step 4 with the rest of the tortillas.

9. Cover with Spicy Tomato Sauce; bake in oven for 10 minutes at 375°.

Prep time: 10 minutes
Cook time: 20 minutes

Nutrients per serving: Calories: 406, Total Fat: 8 g, Sat. Fat: 1 g, Carbs: 71 g, Fiber: 5 g, Sugars: 1 g, Protein: 14 g, Sodium: 350 mg, Cholesterol: 0 mg

Roasted Vegetable Flatbread

I like sandwiches that serve as a complete meal on a bun or flatbread. This sandwich is a balanced combination of healthy fat, carbohydrates and proteins. The more colorful the vegetables, the more antioxidants you will add to your sandwich. Antioxidants help to reduce the ill-effects of stress on your body. The effects of stress include premature aging, blood vessel damage, anxiety and the inability to sleep, to name a few. Makes 4 Sandwiches.

2-4 pieces of whole wheat Flatbread

1 cup of hummus

1 cup of baby arugula

1-2 cups of your favorite roasted vegetables (see the roasted vegetable recipe)

Here's an example of mine:

1/2 cup of red onions

1/2 cup of red bell pepper

1/2 cup of mushrooms

1 cup of zucchini

1. Take one piece of flatbread and cover the entire surface with hummus.
2. On one half of the flatbread add your favorite roasted vegetables. I recommend onions, red bell pepper, mushrooms, and zucchini.
3. Fold over the second half of the flatbread and use the hummus stick it to the vegetables.
4. Cut in half and serve.

Prep time: 10 minutes

Nutrients per serving: Calories: 305, Total Fat: 12 g, Sat. Fat: 2 g, Carbs: 42 g, Fiber: 4 g, Sugars: 2 g, Protein: 8 g, Sodium: 408 mg, Cholesterol: 0 mg

Taco Tuesday

My brother and his family love taco Tuesdays and we always eat them vegetarian style.
Vegetarian tacos are loaded with antioxidants and healthy fiber. The toppings have a combination of fiber and phytonutrients to support anti-aging, and reduce chronic diseases like heart disease, high cholesterol, and diabetes.
Makes 8 servings.

1 teaspoon of olive oil

1/2 cup of red onions, diced

1/2 cup of green bell peppers, diced

1/4 cup of cilantro, chopped

1 teaspoon of cumin

1/2 teaspoon of sea salt

1/2 teaspoon of black pepper

4 garlic cloves, minced

1 1/2 cups of black beans or (15 ounce can, drained)

1 cup of corn kernels

1/2 of lime, fresh squeezed

8 crispy tacos or soft tacos

Toppings:

1 cup of romaine lettuce, shredded

1 cup of tomatoes, diced

1 cup of guacamole - see recipe

1 cup of lime cilantro rice or leftover rice

*1 cup of vegan cheese - optional

2 cups of piquant tomato sauce

1. Add oil to sauce pan over medium heat; then add, onions, bell peppers, cilantro, cumin, salt and black pepper. Sauté for 4 minutes.
2. Add garlic, black beans, corn and heat for another 4 minutes.
3. Remove from heat and add lime juice.
4. Fill the taco shell with the taco filling and add your favorite toppings.
5. Top with 1 teaspoon of the piquant tomato sauce and serve.

Nutrients per serving: Calories: 317, Total Fat: 7 g, Sat. Fat: 1 g, Carbs: 55 g, Fiber: 5 g, Sugars: 3 g, Protein: 12 g, Sodium: 300 mg, Cholesterol: 0 mg

Lime Coconut Chickpeas

This dish is unique because it incorporates fiber and protein into your meal through the use of one ingredient made from tofu--Shirataki noodles. You'll create a meal that is perfect for balancing blood sugars and aids in weight loss without losing taste and flavor. The turmeric in the curry is anti-inflammatory and perfect for anti-aging and heart disease. Yes, there is a little raw sugar but it is needed to balance flavors. You can use agave as a raw sugar substitute. Makes 6 servings.

1/4 cup of canned coconut milk

Juice of one fresh lime (or other citrus on hand)

2 tablespoons of raw sugar

3/4 teaspoon of ground ginger

3/4 teaspoon of garlic powder

1 tablespoon of fresh basil, finely chopped

1/2 teaspoon of salt

1 teaspoon of freshly ground black pepper

1/2 teaspoon of turmeric

1 teaspoon of coconut oil

1 cup of carrots, sliced

1/2 cup of onions, cut lengthwise

2 cups of broccoli

1 cup of chickpeas

*2 cups of cooked angel hair pasta (Consider using Shirataki noodles. They have more fiber and protein than regular noodles or wheat noodles).

1. In a bowl, add coconut milk, lime juice, sugar, ginger, garlic, basil, sea salt, black pepper and turmeric.
2. Whisk until mixed well.
3. In a saucepan, add the coconut oil, carrots and onions; sauté for 3-4 minutes.
4. Add the broccoli, chickpeas, and noodles to the saucepan. Also add the curry sauce to the pan.
5. Simmer for 10 minutes.
6. Serve.

Nutrients per serving: Calories: 183, Total Fat: 8 g, Sat. Fat: 6 g, Carbs: 24 g, Fiber: 4 g, Sugars: 4 g, Protein: 6 g, Sodium: 31 mg, Cholesterol: 13 mg

Sweet and Sassy Chickpea Soubios

Tomatoes and chickpeas have been shown to help lower cholesterol and lower triglycerides. Chickpeas also have a positive effect on modulating appetite. They have also been shown to support insulin release so they balance blood sugars and help with weight loss. Makes 6 servings.

2 teaspoons of olive oil

2 cups of onions, sliced

2 cups of cherry tomatoes, sliced in halves

3-4 tablespoons of fresh ginger minced

1 1/2 cup of chickpeas (15 ounce can, drained)

1/4 cup of fresh cilantro, chopped

1/4 teaspoon of Bragg's Liquid Aminos

1. Place olive oil in the pan on medium heat; add onions. Cook for 20 minutes until the onions start to caramelize. They may turn brown in color - this is normal.
2. In another saucepan, add olive oil, tomatoes, ginger and chickpeas; let simmer for 10 minutes.
3. Once the onions are caramelized add them to the chickpea mixture.
4. Remove from heat and add cilantro and Bragg's Amino Acids
5. Put on a plate and serve with lime mint brown rice.

Prep time: 5 minutes
Cook time: 30 minutes

Nutrients per serving: Calories: 109, Total Fat: 3 g, Sat. Fat: 0 g, Carbs: 18 g, Fiber: 4 g, Sugars: 5 g, Protein: 5 g, Sodium: 14 mg, Cholesterol: 0 mg

"I like a cook who smiles out loud when he tastes his own work.
Let God worry about your modesty; I want to see your enthusiasm."
Robert Farrar Capon

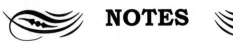

NOTES

Whole Grains Goodness

Butternut Squash Risotto

What I love about risotto is that it has a creamy texture and you don't have to use dairy! Butternut squash is high in beta carotene--the pre-cursor to vitamin A--and is essential for cell repair. It has high amounts of vitamin C as well as antioxidant and anti-inflammatory properties. The key to anti-aging and anti-stress is to reduce damage to cells, so the more anti-oxidants like beta carotene, the better for the anti-aging process. Makes 6 servings.

1 butternut squash, peeled and diced

3 tablespoons of extra virgin olive oil

1/4 teaspoon of sea salt

1/4 teaspoon fresh ground pepper

1/4 teaspoon fresh ground nutmeg

1 whole head of garlic

8 cups of vegetable broth

1/2 cup of shallots

1 1/2 cup of Arborio rice - washed and patted dry

Pinch of saffron threads

1 teaspoon of lemon juice

1/4 cup of parsley

1/2 cup of pine nuts

1. Preheat the oven to 375°.
2. Cover a baking sheet with parchment paper.
3. In a bowl, toss the squash, 1 1/2 tablespoon of extra virgin olive oil, sea salt, pepper, and nutmeg until well coated.
4. Place the squash on parchment paper; bake for 40-50 minutes or until the squash is tender.
5. Cut off the head of garlic and let it roast alongside the squash. Remove from the oven.
6. In a 2 quart pot, bring vegetable broth to a boil; reduce heat to keep broth warm.
7. Puree the squash with 1 cup of the vegetable broth; set aside to add once the risotto is cooked.
8. Let the garlic cool; then mince 3 cloves.
9. In a large saucepan over medium heat, add 1 tablespoon of olive oil.
10. Add shallots and roasted garlic; sauté for 3-5 minutes.
11. Add rice; toast for 3 minutes.
12. Add 1/2 cup of vegetable broth and a pinch of saffron threads.

(continued on next page)

13. Cook down until the broth has evaporated; add another 1/2 cup of vegetable broth. Continue until rice is tender (about 20 minutes).
14. Add lemon juice; stir.
15. Add pureed butternut squash; stir until well mixed.
16. Add chopped parsley and pine nuts. Serve immediately.

Prep time: 10 minutes
Bake time: 40-50 minutes
Cook time: 35 minutes

Nutrients per serving: Calories: 252, Total Fat: 6 g, Sat. Fat: 1 g, Carbs: 48 g, Fiber: 3 g, Sugars: 5 g, Protein: 4 g, Sodium: 310 mg, Cholesterol: 0 mg

"We struggle with eating healthily, obesity, and access to good nutrition for everyone. But we have a great opportunity to get on the right side of this battle by beginning to think differently about the way that we eat and the way that we approach food."
Marcus Samuelsson

Wild Rice with Roasted Nuts

Wild rice is different from white or brown rice. It is actually the seed of a marsh grass. It's unique flavor and texture provides a special complement to your meals. It is high in B vitamins, especially niacin, riboflavin and thiamine. If you're feeling stressed, the B complex vitamins in wild rice is the perfect food to give you a boost. Makes 6 servings.

3/4 cup of wild rice

1 teaspoon of extra virgin olive oil

2 cups of organic vegetable stock*

1 tablespoon of rosemary leaves, chopped

3 garlic cloves, chopped

1/2 cup of pecans

1 tablespoon of flaxseed oil

1. In a saucepan, add wild rice, olive oil, vegetable stock, rosemary and garlic. Bring to a boil, cover and reduce heat. Simmer for 55 minutes.
2. In another saucepan, add pecans and roast on medium heat for about 5 minutes. Constantly stir to prevent burning.
3. Once the rice is fully cooked, add the toasted pecans and flaxseed oil.

Prep time: 5 minutes
Cook time: 1 hour
*If you are choosing a gluten-free diet, check the vegetable stock to make sure there is no gluten in it.

Nutrients per serving: Calories: 165, Total Fat: 10 g, Sat. Fat: 1 g, Carbs: 17 g, Fiber: 2 g, Sugars: 1 g, Protein: 6 g, Sodium: 2 mg, Cholesterol: 0 mg

"You are what what you eat eats."
Michael Pollan, In Defense of Food: An Eater's Manifesto

Simply Barley

Barley is a grain that contains gluten, so this recipe is not appropriate for gluten-free diets. Barley has a nutty flavor and is high in beta glucans that helps to lower cholesterol levels. It's a perfect grain for anyone who is dealing with high cholesterol or heart disease. It is also helpful for easing irritable bowel syndrome and constipation issues. Makes 6 servings.

1 cup of water	1/2 cup of scallions, chopped
2 cups of organic vegetable stock	1/4 cup of celery, chopped
1 cup of pearled barley	5-6 button mushrooms, sliced
1 teaspoon of extra virgin olive oil	1/2 teaspoon of sea salt
	1/4 teaspoon of black pepper

1. In a medium saucepan, bring the vegetable stock and water to a boil over high heat.
2. Add the barley. Reduce heat to a simmer, cover and cook until tender-- about 50 minutes.
3. Place in a large bowl.
4. In a medium skillet, heat oil; add scallions and celery. Cook until the celery is crisp-tender, 5-6 minutes, stirring occasionally.
5. Add the mushrooms, salt and pepper; cook about 5 minutes.
6. Stir the cooked vegetables into the barley. Mix well.

Prep time: 6 minutes
Cook time: 1 hour

Nutrients per serving: Calories: 144, Total Fat: 1 g, Sat. Fat: 0 g, Carbs: 31 g, Fiber: 5 g, Sugars: 1 g, Protein: 3 g, Sodium: 87 mg, Cholesterol: 0 mg

Nutty Rice with Mushrooms

Brown rice is a whole grain because it has fiber along with the starch portion of the grain. The fiber portion of grains contain the trace nutrients our cells and our bodies need. This rice mixed with nuts is a great balance of proteins and carbohydrates. Mushrooms are known to support a healthy immune system. Makes 8 servings.

2 1/2 cups of water	1/2 cup of pecans
1 cup of long grain brown rice	1/2 cup of almonds
2 tablespoons of sunflower oil	1/2 teaspoon of sea salt
1/2 cup of onions, chopped	1/2 teaspoon of black pepper
3 cups of mushrooms, sliced	Pinch of cayenne pepper
1/2 cup of hazelnuts	4 tablespoons of fresh flat leaf parsley, chopped

1. Add rice to boiling water and cook for 35-40 minutes or until tender.
2. Heat 2 tablespoons of oil in a wok or big pan. Add onions and mushrooms; cook for 4 minutes.
3. Add hazelnuts, pecans and almonds; stir-fry for 2 minutes.
4. Mix the rice, salt, pepper, cayenne pepper and parsley. Serve.

Prep time: 5 minutes
Cook time: 45 minutes

Nutrients per serving: Calories: 279, Total Fat: 17 g, Sat. Fat: 1 g, Carbs: 29 g, Fiber: 5 g, Sugars: 2 g, Protein: 6 g, Sodium: 67 mg, Cholesterol: 0 mg

'Cause it's just that good Corn Salad

This is a great potluck salad because it can sit at room temperature without spoiling. Corn is a grain that has a combination of soluble and insoluble fiber, so it stabilizes blood sugar and cholesterol levels at the same time. Surprisingly, corn has many different antioxidant properties differing depending on the color of the corn (white, blue, yellow, red, pink, black, purple). Eating corn can be good for your heart, diabetes and stress management. Makes 6 servings.

1/2 cup of green bell peppers, finely chopped

1/2 cup of onions, finely chopped

2 cups of corn (about 4 ears of corn cooked or grilled and cut off the cob)

2 tablespoons of extra virgin olive oil

1 teaspoon of cumin

2 tablespoons of fresh cilantro

Juice of 1/2 lime

1/2 teaspoon of sea salt

1 garlic clove, finely chopped

1. Mix all ingredients in a large bowl and toss well. Make sure to coat all the ingredients well.

Prep time: 5 minutes (10 minutes if you are cutting corn off the cobb).

Nutrients per serving: Calories: 63, Total Fat: 7 g, Sat. Fat: 1 g, Carbs: 0 g, Fiber: 0 g, Sugars: 0 g, Protein: 0 g, Sodium: 59 mg, Cholesterol: 0 mg

Brown Rice with Beans

The cuisine of many traditional cultures use various combinations of beans and rice. The combination of beans and rice give us what is called a complete protein. Complete proteins contain all the amino acids our bodies need to handle its daily functions. In addition to helping with daily functions, the protein and fiber helps to reduce the risk of heart disease, diabetes and obesity in comparison to eating meat protein.
Makes 6 servings.

1 cup of long grain brown rice, rinsed

1/2 cup of onions, finely chopped

3 garlic cloves, minced

1 1/2 cups of vegetable broth

1/2 cup of water

1 1/2 cups of cooked white beans (15 ounce can, drained)

1. Place rice in a large pot and sauté for 3-4 minutes.
2. Add onions, garlic, vegetable broth, and water; bring to a boil.
3. Cover and reduce to a simmer. Cook 30 minutes.
4. Add white beans and cook for another 5 -10 minutes or until water is absorbed.

Prep time: 5 minutes
Cook time: 40 minutes

Nutrients per serving: Calories: 209, Total Fat: 1 g, Sat. Fat: 0 g, Carbs: 42 g, Fiber: 5 g, Sugars: 1 g, Protein: 7 g, Sodium: 8 mg, Cholesterol: 0 mg

Cornbread Dressing

Cornbread has more fiber and more tasty texture than white bread dressing. Corn is a grain that has a combination of soluble and insoluble fiber, so it stabilizes blood sugar and cholesterol levels at the same time. Makes 12 servings.

8 cups of cornbread

3 tablespoons of vegan butter or extra virgin olive oil

1 1/2 cup of onions, finely chopped

3/4 cup of celery, finely chopped

1/2 cup of carrots, finely chopped

1 tablespoon of dried thyme

1 teaspoon of dried sage

1/2 teaspoon of sea salt

1 teaspoon of black pepper

1 1/2 cup of organic vegetable stock

1. Cut cornbread into 1-inch cubes and place on a large baking sheet. Let it "stale" for several hours or overnight. Place in a large mixing bowl and set aside.
2. Preheat oven to 350°F.
3. In a large skillet, heat vegan butter or oil over medium-low heat.
4. Add onion, celery and carrots; cook, stirring frequently, until softened but not browned.
5. Stir in thyme, sage, salt and pepper.
6. Add mixture to cornbread and toss to blend. Slowly pour in stock; toss to moisten.
7. Spread the stuffing in a buttered or oiled 9x15-inch baking dish. Cover and bake for 20 minutes.
8. Uncover and bake for an additional 20 minutes or until the top is crisp and golden.

Prep time: 10 minutes
Cook time: 5 minutes
Bake time: 40 minutes

Nutrients per serving: Calories: 100, Total Fat: 4 g, Sat. Fat: 1 g, Carbs: 14 g, Fiber: 3 g, Sugars: 2 g, Protein: 2 g, Sodium: 299 mg, Cholesterol: 0 mg

Butternut Squash with Quinoa

Like winter squash, Butternut has been showing up more in grocery stores. It has antioxidant and anti-inflammatory properties that support the repair of chronic illnesses like heart disease, diabetes, and anti-aging.
I paired it with quinoa to have a complete protein in this sweet and savory dish. If you can't find quinoa, you can substitute couscous and cook for less time (5 minutes), but the recipe will no longer be gluten-free. Makes 6 servings.

1 tablespoon of extra virgin olive oil

1/2 cup of yellow onions, diced

3 garlic cloves, minced

1 tablespoon of fresh ginger, minced

3/4 cup of golden raisins

2 cups of butternut squash, peeled and diced small

1/2 teaspoon of sea salt

3 cups of water

1 cup of quinoa, rinsed

3 tablespoons of fresh parsley, chopped

1/2 teaspoon of fresh nutmeg, chopped

1/2 cup of sliced almond

1. In a large saucepan, heat the oil; add onion, garlic and ginger. Cook for 4 minutes.
2. Add raisins; cook another 2 minutes.
3. Add squash and salt; heat over high heat for 2 minutes.
4. Add water. Bring to a boil for about 10 minutes.
5. Reduce heat to a simmer; cook uncovered for 25 minutes or until squash is tender.
6. Once the squash is tender, stir in quinoa, parsley and nutmeg.
7. Cover and cook for another 10 minutes or until water is absorbed and quinoa is done.
8. Remove from heat and fluff the quinoa.
9. Sprinkle almonds over and serve.

Prep time: 16 minutes
Cook time: 55 minutes

Nutrients per serving: Calories: 181, Total Fat: 8 g, Sat. Fat: 1 g, Carbs: 25 g, Fiber: 4 g, Sugars: 11 g, Protein: 5 g, Sodium: 65 mg, Cholesterol: 0 mg

Pasta Medley

Whole wheat pasta has more fiber than regular pasta, so it can have a greater health impact. The healthy oils, proteins and vegetables in this recipe are reminiscent of a meal from a Mediterranean diet. These ingredients have been proven to help with weight loss, improve diabetes, heart disease, cholesterol, and hypertension among other diseases. Makes 6 servings.

1 cup of whole wheat pasta

2 tablespoons of extra virgin olive oil

8 garlic cloves, minced

1/2 cup of shallots, chopped

1/2 teaspoon of sea salt or more to taste

1 teaspoon of black pepper or more to taste

3/4 cup of carrots, chopped

3/4 cup of asparagus, chopped

3/4 cup of zucchini or summer squash, chopped

3/4 cup of fresh parsley, chopped

1 cup of pine nuts

1 fresh lemon, squeezed

1. In a 4-quart pan, add water and bring to a boil. Add whole wheat pasta and cook until tender, about 8-11 minutes.
2. Remove from heat, drain and rinse with cold water to stop the cooking process.
3. In a medium sauté pan, add 1 tablespoon of olive oil, garlic, shallots, salt and pepper; cook for 2 minutes.
4. Add carrots, asparagus and zucchini or summer squash. Cook vegetables for 5 minutes or until tender.
5. Remove from the heat and mix with the remaining olive oil, cooked pasta, lemon juice, fresh parsley and pine nuts.

Prep time: 15 minutes
Cook time: 18 minutes

Nutrients per serving: Calories: 79, Total Fat: 5 g, Sat. Fat: 1 g, Carbs: 9 g, Fiber: 1 g, Sugars: 2 g, Protein: 2 g, Sodium: 98 mg, Cholesterol: 0 mg

Lime Cilantro Brown Rice

Brown rice is a whole grain because it has fiber along with the starch portion of the grain. The fiber portion of grains contain the trace nutrients our cells and our bodies need. A large Harvard study concluded that women who eat all whole grains like brown rice weighed less than those who did not.
Makes 6 servings.

1 1/2 cup of water
1 cup of long grain brown rice (rinsed)
1/4 cup of lime juice

1/2 cup of cilantro, chopped
1 teaspoon of sea salt
1/2 cup of scallions

1. Add rice to boiling water; cook for 35-40 minutes or until water has completely evaporated.
2. Pour into a bowl and fluff with a fork; allow to cool.
3. Add lime juice, cilantro, salt and scallions.
4. Serve.

Prep time: 5 minutes
Cook time: 45 minutes

Nutrients per serving: Calories: 150, Total Fat: 1 g, Sat. Fat: 0 g, Carbs: 31 g, Fiber: 3 g, Sugars: 1 g, Protein: 4 g, Sodium: 87 mg, Cholesterol: 0 mg

"I like a cook who smiles out loud when he tastes his own work.
Let God worry about your modesty; I want to see your enthusiasm."
Robert Farrar Capon

NOTES

Vibrant Vegetables

Vegetarian Collard Greens

Here is the secret to great tasting greens. Add an acid like lemon or vinegar at the end of cooking and it enhances the flavor and makes them tender and delicious!
Greens, like collards, belong to the cruciferous vegetable family are known for cholesterol lowering effects as one of their healing properties. They are also exceptional in supporting the detoxification process to remove toxins from the body. Eat them several times per week if possible. Makes 8 servings.

1 bunch fresh collard greens

2 tablespoons of extra virgin olive oil

Sea salt and pepper, to taste

1 medium yellow onion, chopped

6-8 garlic cloves, crushed

1 cup of vegetable broth

Juice of 1/2 lemon

2-3 tablespoons of rice wine vinegar

Pinch of cayenne pepper (optional)

1. Clean the collard greens and strip them from the stalk.
2. Stack 5 or 6 leaves on top of one another and roll them up so they look like a green cigar. Cut across the cigar to make thin strips.
3. In a large pot, over medium heat, add the olive oil, salt, pepper and chopped onions. Sauté until onions are translucent.
4. Add garlic, collard greens and vegetable broth. If you are adding cayenne pepper add it now.
5. Simmer on medium-low heat for 25 minutes, stirring occasionally to make sure that the greens are cooking evenly.
6. Add lemon juice and vinegar, and cook for another 15 minutes or until greens are tender.

Prep time: 20 minutes
Cook time: 45 minutes

Nutrients per serving: Calories: 49, Total Fat: 4 g, Sat. Fat: 1 g, Carbs: 4 g, Fiber: 1 g, Sugars: 1 g, Protein: 1 g, Sodium: 74 mg, Cholesterol: 0 mg

Sweet Sautéed Kale

One of my favorite traits of kale is that it's fast to prepare! Kale is one of the most versatile greens in the cruciferous vegetable family! It has one of the highest levels of calcium of any green leafy vegetable. Enjoy kale and get your calcium--it's good for your bones and your heart. Makes 4 servings.

1 bunch of kale, washed

1/2 cup of yellow onions, chopped

2 tablespoons of extra virgin olive oil

4 garlic cloves, chopped

Pinch of sea salt

Pinch of black pepper

2 tablespoons of balsamic vinegar

1. De-rib kale and tear into bite-sized pieces.
2. In a sauce pan, add oil, onions and garlic. Cook for 1 minute.
3. Add kale, salt and pepper. Cook for 4 minutes.
4. Turn off the heat and pour vinegar over kale.

Prep time: 10 minutes
Cook time: 5 minutes

Nutrients per serving: Calories: 115, Total Fat: 1 g, Sat. Fat: 0 g, Carbs: 11 g, Fiber: 2 g, Sugars: 2 g, Protein: 3 g, Sodium: 32 mg, Cholesterol: 0 mg

"When walking, walk. When eating, eat." rashaski • Zen Proverb

Savory Sweet Potatoes

Sweet potatoes can be eaten sweet or savory. In this case, they are savory and quite delicious! Since sweet potatoes have phytonutrients, they are anti-inflammatory, blood sugar balancing, and anti-aging. Prepare and eat them in many different ways. Makes 4 servings.

2 small-medium sweet potatoes

1 small yellow onion

2 tablespoons of extra virgin olive oil

1/2 teaspoon of sea salt

1/4 teaspoon of pepper

2 garlic cloves, crushed

1. Wash the sweet potatoes with a vegetable brush and set aside.
2. Set the food processor with the julienne fixture.
3. Julienne the sweet potatoes in the food processor; remove to a separate bowl. If you don't have a food processor just grate the sweet potatoes.
4. Repeat the same procedure for the onions.
5. In a medium saucepan, add the oil, salt, pepper, garlic and onions; sauté for 2 minutes.
6. Add sweet potatoes and gently stir to make sure they are coated with oil.
7. Continue cooking until sweet potatoes are tender, about 5 minutes.

Prep time: 7 minutes
Cook time: 7 minutes

Nutrients per serving: Calories: 64, Total Fat: 2 g, Sat. Fat: 0 g, Carbs: 10 g, Fiber: 2 g, Sugars: 2 g, Protein: 1 g, Sodium: 102 mg, Cholesterol: 0 mg

Minty Summer Squash

Include summer squash in all your favorite mixed vegetable dishes or make a simple light meal like this one. Summer squash has high amounts of B vitamins and special fiber called pectin that is important in balancing blood sugars. This is important for maintaining energy, weight and normal blood sugars. Makes 4 servings.

2 summer squash

1/2 teaspoon of sea salt

1 tablespoon of extra virgin olive oil

2 garlic cloves, chopped

2 tablespoons of fresh spearmint, minced

Freshly ground black pepper to taste

1. Cut off the bottoms and stems of the squash. Cut the squash lengthwise into small pieces, about 1/8-inch wide.
2. Sprinkle squash with salt; let stand for 15 minutes.
3. Gently squeeze the squash to release the excess water.
4. In a medium sauté pan, add the olive oil and garlic; sauté for about 1 minute.
5. Add spearmint and drained squash; cook for another minute. Serve immediately.

Prep time: 20 minutes
Cook time: 2-3 minutes

Nutrients per serving: Calories: 50, Total Fat: 4 g, Sat. Fat: 1 g, Carbs: 4 g, Fiber: 1 g, Sugars: 2 g, Protein: 1 g, Sodium: 128 mg, Cholesterol: 0 mg

Sautéed Cabbage

This is another member of the cruciferous vegetable family so it has numerous anti-cancer properties. Cabbage is supportive for healing the digestive tract and digestive disorders. It contains high amounts of the amino acid glutamine that heals the digestive tract. So consider eating sautéed cabbage when you are having digestive issues. Makes 6 servings.

1 teaspoon of extra virgin olive oil

1 head of cabbage, shredded

4 garlic cloves, minced

2 teaspoons of white wine vinegar

1/2 cup of vegetable broth

1 teaspoon of chopped chives

1/2 teaspoon of cumin

1. In a large skillet, sauté cabbage in oil for 3 minutes.
2. Add garlic, vegetable broth, vinegar, chives and cumin.
3. Cook covered for 10-15 minutes.

Prep time: 7 minutes
Cook time: 13 minutes

Nutrients per serving: Calories: 41, Total Fat: 1 g, Sat. Fat: 0 g, Carbs: 8 g, Fiber: 3 g, Sugars: 4 g, Protein: 2 g, Sodium: 68 mg, Cholesterol: 0 mg

Steamed Broccoli with a Twist

The lemon gives this dish a wonderful twist. Broccoli is the member cruciferous vegetable family that supports the liver detoxification system. When broccoli is steamed is fiber-related components bind with the bile from the liver and gallbladder of digestive tract. This helps with lowering cholesterol levels. Makes 4 servings.

1/2 cup of water
1 bunch broccoli, stemmed
 and chopped
2 teaspoons of extra virgin
 olive oil

Juice of 1 lemon, freshly
 squeezed
1/4 teaspoon of sea salt

1. Pour water in the bottom of a pan.
2. Place steamer on the bottom of the pan. Place broccoli on the steamer. If you don't have a steamer then just put the broccoli in with the water. Cover the pan.
3. Over medium-low heat, steam for 5-7 minutes or until you can pierce the broccoli easily.
4. Put on plate and sprinkle lemon, olive oil and sea salt over top and serve.

Prep time: 5 minutes
Cook time: 5 minutes

Nutrients per serving: Calories: 74, Total Fat: 3 g, Sat. Fat: 0 g, Carbs: 11 g, Fiber: 4 g, Sugars: 3 g, Protein: 4 g, Sodium: 168 mg, Cholesterol: 0 mg

"Tell me what you eat, and I will tell you who you are."
Brillat-Savarin

Basically Fantastic Brussels Sprouts

You guessed it, the cruciferous vegetable family strikes again! All cruciferous vegetables have anti-inflammatory, antioxidant and anti-cancer properties. They also help with detoxification and digestive support. Brussels sprouts are being studied for their ability to protect our DNA from damage. This is important for anti-aging and cancer prevention. Cutting the Brussels sprouts into thin slices changes the flavor and your entire experience of them. Makes 6 servings.

1 pound of Brussels sprouts

1 tablespoons of extra virgin olive oil

2 large shallots, thinly sliced

2 teaspoons of fresh lime juice

1 teaspoon of dill leaves, chopped

Sea salt and pepper to taste

1. Rinse Brussels sprouts and remove discolored leaves.
2. Cut sprouts in half and thinly slice lengthwise.
2. Add olive oil in a heavy skillet over medium high heat.
3. Add sprouts and shallots; stir-fry until tender and lightly browned, about 8 minutes.
4. Remove from heat and transfer to a large bowl.
5. Drizzle with fresh lime juice, season with sea salt, dill and pepper; toss.

Prep time: 6 minutes
Cook time: 8 minutes

Nutrients per serving: Calories: 137, Total Fat: 3 g, Sat. Fat: 0 g, Carbs: 25 g, Fiber: 9 g, Sugars: 5 g, Protein: 8 g, Sodium: 61 mg, Cholesterol: 0 mg

Fruit-Filled Acorn Squash

This dish is so sweet that it could be mistaken for dessert.
It's a great side dish. Acorn squash, apples and pears all have
antioxidant and anti-inflammatory properties. The squash also
has insulin-regulating properties to regulate blood sugars.
The cinnamon and fiber helps to balance blood sugars too.
This recipe is great for diabetics and pre-diabetics as well.
Makes 8 servings.

2 acorn squash

2 apples, peeled, cored and diced

1 pear, peeled, cored and diced

1/4 cup of raisins

1/4 cup of orange juice

1 tablespoon of turbinado sugar or agave nectar

1/2 teaspoon of cinnamon

1/4 teaspoon of nutmeg

2 tablespoons of sunflower oil

Mint sprigs

1. Preheat the oven to 325°.
2. Cut the acorn squash into halves; remove the seeds. Pour 1/4 cup of water into a baking dish and place squash cut-side down. Remove the squash from the baking dish and pierce with a fork in several places.
3. Bake for 45 minutes or until tender. Let cool slightly while preparing the filling.
4. In a bowl, combine apples, pears, raisins, turbinado sugar, cinnamon and nutmeg.
5. Place vegetable oil in a saucepan. Add the ingredients from the bowl and cook uncovered for about 5 minutes using medium heat.
6. Add orange juice; cook until the ingredients are soft, about 5 minutes. Remove from heat.
7. Spoon some of the juice into the warm squash; and add about 1/4 cup of filling.
8. Finish with a sprig of mint and serve.
*To make this a blood sugar balancing recipe, use agave nectar instead of turbinado sugar.

Prep time: 15 minutes
Cook time: 10 minutes
Bake time: 45 minutes

Nutrients per serving: Calories: 98, Total Fat: 0 g, Sat. Fat: 0 g, Carbs: 25 g, Fiber: 4 g, Sugars: 11 g, Protein: 1 g, Sodium: 4 mg, Cholesterol: 0 mg

Curried Mixed Greens

Using a combination of green leafy vegetables packs this dish with antioxidant and anti-inflammatory properties. These greens reduce the risk of chronic diseases and supports anti-aging. Roti is similar to a tortilla but it thinner and made with chickpea flour instead of wheat. If you don't have roti you can serve over any rice or grain. Makes 8 servings.

1 1/2 cup of vegetable broth

1 small red onion, diced

2 roasted red peppers, diced

6 garlic cloves, minced

4-5 large leaves of collards greens, cleaned and cut into strips

4-5 large leaves of turnip greens, cleaned and cut into strips

4-5 large leaves of mustard greens, cleaned and cut into strips

3 cups of spinach, cleaned and cut into strips

2 tablespoons of curry powder

1 teaspoon of sea salt

1/4 teaspoon of black pepper

1 cup of diced potatoes

1 1/2 cups of cooked chickpeas, cooked (15 ounce can, drained)

1. Add 1/4 cup of the vegetable broth, red onions, red peppers and garlic to a large sauté pan; boil at low heat for 5 minutes, until soft.
2. Add the collard greens, turnip greens, mustard greens, and spinach, curry powder, salt, pepper, potatoes and the rest of the vegetable broth.
3. Cook for 20 minutes or until potatoes are soft.
4. Add cooked chickpeas and cook for 5 minutes to warm the chickpeas.
5. Lay the roti out like a tortilla and fill the center with the curried mixed greens. Then fold the two sides into the middle covering the filling. Finally roll the roti from the top down to the bottom and enjoy.

Prep time: 20 minutes
Cook time: 30 minutes

Nutrients per serving: Calories: 149, Total Fat: 3 g, Sat. Fat: 0 g, Carbs: 27 g, Fiber: 6 g, Sugars: 4 g, Protein: 6 g, Sodium: 210 mg, Cholesterol: 0 mg

Sweet Swiss Chard

I first fell in love with Swiss chard as an adult because it's easy to prepare and can be eaten raw or cooked. Swiss chard has been shown to have anti-inflammatory and bone health benefits from their nutrients. The blood sugar balancing effects are enhanced by the fiber. Swiss chard has a delicate flavor similar to spinach. Makes 6 servings.

1 bunch of Swiss chard

2 teaspoons of extra virgin olive oil

6 garlic cloves, minced

1/2 cup of red onion, chopped

1/2 cup of yellow bell pepper, chopped

1. De-vein the Swiss chard by pulling the leaves from the stem. Tear the leaves into bite-sized pieces; place them in a large bowl filled with cold water. This will wash dirt from the leaves and help it wilt during cooking.
2. In a sauté pan on medium-low heat, add oil, garlic, red onions and yellow peppers. Sauté for 1 minute.
3. Add the Swiss chard and cook for another 3-4 minutes, turning the chard until it wilts.

Prep time: 10 minutes
Cook time: 5 minutes

Nutrients per serving: Calories: 49, Total Fat: 1 g, Sat. Fat: 0 g, Carbs: 6 g, Fiber: 1 g, Sugars: 1 g, Protein: 1 g, Sodium: 79 mg, Cholesterol: 0 mg

"If you're concerned about your health, you should probably avoid products that make health claims. Why? Because a health claim on a food product is a strong indication it's not really food, and food is what you want to eat"
Michael Pollan, In Defense of Food: An Eater's Manifesto

Roasted Vegetables

Roasting is one of my favorite ways eat vegetables. Once roasted, they can be used in a variety of different ways. The vegetables in this recipe have anti-inflammatory properties and decrease the risk for diabetes, heart disease, auto-immune diseases. Makes 6 servings.

1 red bell pepper, sliced

1 eggplant, cut into disks

1 red onion, sliced

1 zucchini, sliced long way

2 cups of baby bella mushrooms or 4 large portabella

2 tablespoons of extra virgin olive oil

1 teaspoon of sea salt

1 teaspoon of pepper

1. Preheat oven to 400 degrees. Place parchment paper on a cookie sheet.
2. In a bowl, place the vegetables and toss with oil, salt, and pepper.
3. Place vegetables on the cookie sheet.
4. Bake for 30-40 minutes until tender.
5. Remove from the oven and let cool. Serve.

Prep time: 10 minutes
Bake time 40 minutes

Nutrients per serving: Calories: 47, Total Fat: 2 g, Sat. Fat: 0 g, Carbs: 7 g, Fiber: 3 g, Sugars: 3 g, Protein: 2 g, Sodium: 64 mg, Cholesterol: 0 mg

Curried Chard and Potatoes

One of the benefits of curry is the spice turmeric. It's what gives curry it's yellow color. Turmeric is a powerful anti-inflammatory, so it reduces pain and swelling in the body. It also inhibits cancer cell growth (the Swiss chard does too, by the way). It also helps with digestion and digestive problems. At times, I have used spinach instead of the chard and it was just as enjoyable. Play with substituting your favorite greens and vegetables to ramp up the fiber and flavor at the same time. Makes 6 servings.

4 leaves of red or white chard, both stems and leaves

2 cups of water

2 medium red-skinned potatoes, washed and cubed

1 teaspoon of olive oil

1 1/2 teaspoon of curry powder

1/2 teaspoon of ground coriander

1/2 teaspoon of ground cumin

5 garlic cloves, minced

1 teaspoon of sea salt

1/2 teaspoon of black pepper

1/4 teaspoon of cayenne pepper

1. Wash the chard leaves. Remove stems and chop. Tear leaves into bite-sized pieces; set stems and leaves aside separately.
2. Steam potatoes until they are tender, about 8 minutes.
3. Once the potatoes are tender place them in a sauté pan. Add the olive oil, curry powder, coriander, cumin, garlic, salt, black pepper and cayenne pepper and stems of chard and cook for 5 minutes.
4. Add the chard leaves and cook for another 5 minutes.

Prep time: 8 minutes
Cook time: 18 minutes

Nutrients per serving: Calories: 67, Total Fat: 1 g, Sat. Fat: 0 g, Carbs: 14 g, Fiber: 2 g, Sugars: 1 g, Protein: 2 g, Sodium: 160 mg, Cholesterol: 0 mg

Spaghetti Squash Pasta

When cooked correctly, this squash looks like pieces of spaghetti. This is a great way to add fiber to your meal. The cooking process is different based on the size of squash that you choose. My suggestion is that you choose the smallest one that you can find because they yield more than you might think. Makes 8 servings.

1 medium spaghetti squash

Puncture holes in the squash with a knife, making sure to evenly distribute holes over the entire squash.

Microwave instructions: Place in the microwave on high for 15 minutes, turning every 5 minutes to ensure even cooking. Take the squash out of the microwave with oven mitts, it will be hot!

Oven instructions: Place squash on a baking sheet in the oven at 350° for 45-60 minutes or until soft.
1. Let the squash cool for 10 minutes; cut in half.
2. Scoop out the seeds and discard.
3. Scoop out the meat of the squash. It will start to unravel into strings like spaghetti.
4. Top with Tomato Basil Sauce (see recipe) or your favorite spaghetti sauce.

Prep time: 5 minutes
Cook time: 1 hour

Nutrients per serving: Calories: 31, Total Fat: 1 g, Sat. Fat: 0 g, Carbs: 7 g, Fiber: 0 g, Sugars: 0 g, Protein: 1 g, Sodium: 17 mg, Cholesterol: 0 mg

Tomato Basil Sauce

This simple sauce is a great base sauce because you can add your favorite ingredients to it like mushrooms or artichokes. Tomatoes are full of anti-oxidants, vitamins C & E and lycopene that are important for heart health. Lycopene is increased when tomatoes are cooked. Lycopene in particular helps decrease all bad cholesterol markers--total cholesterol, LDL cholesterol, and triglyceride levels. It also supports bone health and has anti-cancer properties. Makes 8 servings.

6 quarts of water

1 teaspoon of sea salt

6 medium tomatoes (or 28 ounce can of diced tomatoes)

3 tablespoons of extra virgin olive oil

3 garlic cloves, chopped

1/3 cup of fresh parsley, chopped

1/3 cup of fresh basil, chopped

2 tablespoons of dried oregano

1/4 teaspoon of sea salt

1/4 teaspoon of pepper

1. Bring water to a boil in a large pot with 1 teaspoon of salt.
2. Carefully drop the tomatoes into the water for 15-30 seconds.
3. Scoop them out and run under cold water. Remove the skin, which should peel off with ease.
4. Cut tomatoes into chunks and set aside.
5. Heat olive oil in a saucepan over medium heat. Add garlic, parsley, basil, oregano, salt and pepper.
6. Add tomatoes and cook on simmer for 20-30 minutes to thicken the sauce.

Prep time: 10 minutes
Cook time: 30 minutes

Nutrients per serving: Calories: 76, Total Fat: 6 g, Sat. Fat: 1 g, Carbs: 6 g, Fiber: 2 g, Sugars: 4 g, Protein: 1 g, Sodium: 67 mg, Cholesterol: 0 mg

Piquant Tomato Sauce

I love this sauce! It is lovely as a base for flatbreads or served over enchiladas. Tomatoes are full of anti-oxidants, vitamins C & E and lycopene and is important to heart health. Lycopene is increased when tomatoes are cooked. Lycopene in particular helps decrease all bad cholesterol markers- total cholesterol, LDL cholesterol, and triglyceride levels. It also supports bone health and has anti-cancer properties. Makes 8 servings.

6 medium tomatoes (or 28 ounce canned diced tomatoes)

1 1/2 tablespoon of extra virgin olive oil

1 cup of onions, chopped

1/2 cup of fresh cilantro, chopped

2 teaspoons of cumin

2 teaspoons of chili powder

1 tablespoon of jalapeno pepper, finely chopped

1/2 teaspoon of sea salt

6 garlic cloves, chopped

1. If using fresh tomatoes, cut tomatoes into chunks and set aside.
2. Heat olive oil in a saucepan over medium heat. Add onions, cilantro, cumin, chili powder, jalapeno, salt and pepper.
3. Add tomatoes and cook on simmer for 15 minutes to let the sauce thicken.
4. Add garlic after 15 minutes.
5. Simmer for another 15 minutes. Turn off heat and serve.

Prep time: 10 minutes
Cook time: 30 minutes

Nutrients per serving: Calories: 42, Total Fat: 3 g, Sat. Fat: 0 g, Carbs: 4 g, Fiber: 1 g, Sugars: 1 g, Protein: 1 g, Sodium: 68 mg, Cholesterol: 0 mg

Mushroom Gravy

There are so many different types of mushrooms you can experiment with to make this gravy. Mushrooms have molecules called long chain polysaccharides that help to support the immune system to fight off disease. You can use this tasty and versatile sauce as gravy over whole grains, nut loaf, or your favorite noodle dish. Makes 8 servings.

1 medium yellow onion, chopped

1 teaspoons of extra virgin olive oil

1/2 teaspoon of sea salt

1/2 teaspoon of crushed black pepper (add up to 1 teaspoon for more spiciness)

3 garlic cloves, minced

1 1/2 cup of mushrooms, chopped (use your favorite)

1 teaspoon of turmeric

1 cup of vegetable broth

2 teaspoons arrowroot (you can substitute with corn starch or wheat flour depending on your pantry)

1. Heat olive oil on medium high; add onions, salt and pepper.
2. Cook for 2 minutes or until the onions become translucent.
3. Reduce heat to medium-low; add garlic, mushrooms and turmeric. Cook until mushrooms are soft.
4. In a small bowl, mix the arrowroot and broth until well combined.
5. Slowly pour the broth and flour mix into the pan, and stir until gravy thickens, about 4-5 minutes.

Prep time: 5 minutes
Cook time: 10 minutes

Nutrients per serving: Calories: 21, Total Fat: 1 g, Sat. Fat: 0 g, Carbs: 4 g, Fiber: 1 g, Sugars: 1 g, Protein: 1 g, Sodium: 71 mg, Cholesterol: 0 mg

Cranberry Relish

Cranberry sauce is a quick dish that adds tangy flavor along with tons of antioxidants. Cranberries are high in antioxidant and anti-inflammatory properties. They are essential for anti-aging and heart health. The fiber supports blood sugar levels to counteract the sugar in the recipe. Makes 8 servings.

2 cups of cranberries

1/2 cup of turbinado sugar

1/2 cup of water

1/2 cup of orange juice

1/2 cup of orange slices, seeded

1. Rinse cranberries in a bowl of water. Pick out any cranberries that are soft or have bad spots.
2. In a large skillet over medium heat, combine the cranberries, sugar, water, and orange juice.
3. Cook for about 10 minutes.
4. The cranberries will start to 'pop' and the liquid will congeal. The longer you cook it the thicker it will be become. I suggest another 5-10 minutes.
5. Remove from heat and add orange slices for texture and flavor.

Prep time: 10 minutes
Cook time: 18 minutes

Nutrients per serving: Calories: 74, Total Fat: 0 g, Sat. Fat: 0 g, Carbs: 19 g, Fiber: 2 g, Sugars: 15 g, Protein: 0 g, Sodium: 1 mg, Cholesterol: 0 mg

"Chocolate is one of the world's most beloved discoveries, and when we need a quick boost of energy and endorphins, chocolate is the go-to treat."
Marcus Samuelsson

Cranberry Relish Plus

Cranberry sauce is one of my favorite thanksgiving side dishes. It can be made quite versatile by adding your favorite fruit and spices. Persimmons and cranberries are both high in vitamin C and they have high antioxidant phytonutrients as well. Persimmons are a seasonal fruit and are usually available in stores and farmers' markets in the fall. The spices in this recipe support blood sugar balancing and digestive health.
Makes 8 servings.

1 cup of fresh cranberries
1/4 cup of orange juice
1/4 cup of water
1/2 cup of turbinado sugar

1 persimmon, chopped or diced
1/4 teaspoon of ground ginger
1/4 cup of walnuts

1. Rinse cranberries in a bowl of water. Pick out any cranberries that are soft or have bad spots.
2. In a 4-quart pan on medium heat, add cranberries, orange juice, water and sugar; simmer for 10 minutes.
3. When the cranberries start to 'pop', add the persimmon and ginger; cook 10 minutes.
4. Turn off heat, add walnuts, and let cool for 30 minutes.

Prep time: 8 minutes
Cook time: 20 minutes

Nutrients per serving: Calories: 100, Total Fat: 2 g, Sat. Fat: 0 g, Carbs: 20 g, Fiber: 2 g, Sugars: 17 g, Protein: 1 g, Sodium: 1 mg, Cholesterol: 0 mg

Roasted Butternut squash

Like winter squash, butternut squash is hearty and delicious for fall. It has antioxidant and anti-inflammatory properties that support the repair of chronic illnesses like heart disease and diabetes. It can be eaten right out of the oven or added to salads, soups, and even risotto (there is a butternut squash risotto recipe in the entrée section of this book).
Makes 8 servings.

1 butternut squash, peeled and diced

1 tablespoon of extra virgin olive oil

1/4 teaspoon of sea salt

1/4 teaspoon of fresh ground pepper

1/4 teaspoon of fresh ground nutmeg

1. Preheat the oven to 375 degrees.
2. Cover a cookie sheet with parchment paper.
3. In a bowl toss the squash, extra virgin olive oil, sea salt, pepper and nutmeg until well coated.
4. Place the squash on parchment paper and bake for 40-50 minutes until the squash is tender.

Prep time: 10 minutes
Bake time 50 minutes

Nutrients per serving: Calories: 63, Total Fat: 2 g, Sat. Fat: 0 g, Carbs: 12 g, Fiber: 2 g, Sugars: 2 g, Protein: 1 g, Sodium: 63 mg, Cholesterol: 0 mg

Roasted Beets

Beets are a great! The greens and roots of the beet are edible. Both are antioxidant, anti-inflammatory and support detoxification. The deep reddish/purple/orange color shows us they are packed with antioxidants to support the repair and restoration of the cells. Beets also have a special property to support liver detoxification. So, anyone who wants to detoxify should add beets to their plan. Makes 8 servings.

6 red beets

1 tablespoons of extra virgin olive oil

1 teaspoon of fresh ginger

1/4 teaspoon of sea salt

1/4 teaspoon of fresh black pepper

1. Preheat the oven to 400 °F.
2. Place parchment paper on a baking sheet and set aside.
3. Wash beets and peel them.
4. Cut them into 1-inch slices and place them in a large bowl.
5. Add the olive oil, ginger, salt, pepper and toss to coat all the pieces well.
6. Place the beets on parchment paper and roast for 40 minutes.

Prep time: 10 minutes
Bake time 40 minutes

Nutrients per serving: Calories: 44, Total Fat: 2 g, Sat. Fat: 0 g, Carbs: 6 g, Fiber: 2 g, Sugars: 4 g, Protein: 1 g, Sodium: 107 mg, Cholesterol: 0 mg

Supercharged Snacks

Traditional Salsa Recipe

Who doesn't love fresh salsa? Once you see how easy it is, you will be hooked on making different types of fruit and vegetable salsas. This salsa is packed with flavors and phytonutrients. Jalapeños and tomatoes have antioxidants essential for tissue repair, anti-aging and heart health. Makes 4 servings.

2 medium tomatoes, diced into small pieces

1/2 of a red onion, diced into small pieces

1/2 of a jalapeño pepper, minced

Juice of 1 lime squeeze

1/2 cup of cilantro, chopped

1/4 teaspoon of sea salt

1/4 teaspoon of black pepper

1/4 teaspoon of cumin

1. Add all the ingredients in a bowl; mix.
2. Refrigerate for one hour.

Prep time: 10 minutes
Chill time: 1 hour

Nutrients per serving: Calories: 19, Total Fat: 0 g, Sat. Fat: 0 g, Carbs: 5 g, Fiber: 1 g, Sugars: 3 g, Protein: 1 g, Sodium: 29 mg, Cholesterol: 0 mg

Pineapple Salsa

Fruit salsas are an excellent way to get an extra serving of fruit and vegetables into your body. Pineapples have a chemical called bromelain, which supports digestion and reduces pain and inflammation. Ginger supports healthy digestion as well. This salsa is extremely delicious and can be used as a snack or a side dish. Makes 4 servings.

1 1/2 cup of fresh pineapple, sliced small

1/4 cup of red onions

Juice of 1 lime, squeezed

1 tablespoon of ginger, minced

1 tablespoon of cilantro

1/2 - 1 teaspoon of jalapeño, minced

1/4 cup of green onions

In a bowl, mix all ingredients together. Chill until ready to serve.

Prep time: 10 minutes
Chill time: 1 hour

Nutrients per serving: Calories: 52, Total Fat: 1 g, Sat. Fat: 0 g, Carbs: 14 g, Fiber: 1 g, Sugars: 7 g, Protein: 1 g, Sodium: 6 mg, Cholesterol: 0 mg

Black Bean Salsa

Salsa doesn't have to be made fruit, you can also use beans for protein. This nutrient dense snack has the combination of protein and fiber that is perfect for balancing blood sugars and satisfying craving in diabetes. It aids in weight loss as well. The soluble fiber also supports digestive and heart health.
Makes 4 servings.

1 1/2 cup of cooked black beans (15 ounce can, drained)

1 cup of corn kernels (fresh or frozen)

1 teaspoon of fresh jalapeño pepper, minced (optional)

2 medium tomatoes, diced

1/3 cup of fresh cilantro, chopped

1/4 cup of red onion, diced

2 limes, freshly squeezed

1 teaspoon of ground cumin

1 teaspoon of sea salt

1 teaspoon of black pepper

Combine all the ingredients in a large bowl. Cover and chill for at least two hours.

Prep time: 10 minutes
Chill time: 2 hours

Nutrients per serving: Calories: 98, Total Fat: 1 g, Sat. Fat: 0 g, Carbs: 20 g, Fiber: 5 g, Sugars: 2 g, Protein: 5 g, Sodium: 84 mg, Cholesterol: 0 mg

Roasted Red Pepper Hummus

Chickpeas are a great snack and when included as part of a healthy diet have been shown to reduce appetite and help with weight loss. They have also been shown to support insulin release so they balance blood sugars and help with weight loss. Makes 6 servings.

1 teaspoon of tahini

1 1/2 cup of chickpeas (15 ounce can, drained)

1/2 teaspoon of sea salt

1 1/2 tablespoon of extra virgin olive oil

1-2 garlic cloves

1/4 cup of roasted red peppers

1 juice of 1 lemon

1. In the bowl of a food processor, add tahini, chickpeas, salt, oil, garlic, roasted peppers, and lemon juice.
2. Blend for 1 minute or until smooth.
3. Enjoy with raw vegetables, or whole grain crackers.

Prep time: 5 minutes

Nutrients per serving: Calories: 162, Total Fat: 7 g, Sat. Fat: 1 g, Carbs: 19 g, Fiber: 5 g, Sugars: 4 g, Protein: 6 g, Sodium: 123 mg, Cholesterol: 0 mg

"Getting as much sleep as possible and following a healthy diet will stop you from feeling run-down if, like me, you're super-stressed."
Elizabeth Hurley

Super Simple Guacamole

Guacamole can be used as a snack or a topping for salads, soups, or anything with black beans. This simple guacamole is great because avocados are a wonderful source of good fat. Avocadoes have incredible healing properties that range from anti-inflammatory, to heart health, to blood sugar balancing.
Makes 6 servings.

2 ripe avocadoes, peeled
Juice of 1 lime
1/4 cup of red onion, diced
1 garlic clove, minced
1/8 teaspoon of cumin

1/4 teaspoon of sea salt
1/4 cup of fresh cilantro, chopped
3 fresh red chilies, diced (optional)
1/2 cup of tomatoes, chopped

1. Mash the avocados in a bowl.
2. Add lime juice, onion, garlic, cumin, salt, cilantro and chilies. Mix well.
3. Gently mix in the tomatoes.

Prep time: 5 minutes

Nutrients per serving: Calories: 116, Total Fat: 10 g, Sat. Fat: 0g, Carbs: 8 g, Fiber: 5 g, Sugars: 1 g, Protein: 2 g, Sodium: 85 mg, Cholesterol: 0 mg

Roasted pumpkin seeds

Have you ever thought about the power of seeds? Seeds have all the information, vitamins and nutrients required to make a plant grow. When we add seeds to our snacks and meals we are getting the small and potent goodness of nature. Pumpkin seeds have high amounts of vitamin E and anti-oxidants for cell protection and repair. They've been studied for their ability to help with enlarged prostate issues and prostate cancer. They are good for kids as well as adults. This is a great fall snack that your kids can help make. Makes 4-6 servings.

Pumpkin seeds from one pumpkins

1 teaspoons of extra virgin olive oil

1/2 - 1 teaspoon sea salt

1. Pre-heat oven to 400° F.
2. Take seeds out of a pumpkin and remove all of the webbing.
3. Rinse pumpkin seeds under water to remove the meat and webbing from the seeds.
4. Pat dry.
5. Place seeds in a bowl with oil and salt; toss thoroughly.
6. Place on parchment paper on a baking sheet.
7. Place pumpkin seeds on the parchment paper.
8. Bake pumpkin seeds for 10 minutes.

Prep time: 5 minutes
Bake time: 10 minutes

Nutrients per serving: Calories: 81, Total Fat: 4 g, Sat. Fat: 1g, Carbs: 9 g, Fiber: 0 g, Sugars: 0 g, Protein: 3 g, Sodium: 120 mg, Cholesterol: 0 mg

Glazed Almonds

Sweet and salty flavor combinations are a favorite of many people. The great thing about glazed almonds is you can carry them with you anywhere. Almonds have been studied for lowering 'bad' cholesterol as well as for protection from diabetes and heart disease. So eat up! Makes 6 servings.

1 cup of raw almonds

1/4- 1/2 cup of dried cranberries

1/8 cup of agave nectar

1/2 teaspoon of real vanilla extract

A pinch of cayenne pepper

2 tablespoons of sesame seeds

1/4 teaspoon of sea salt

1. Preheat the oven to 325°F.
2. In a bowl add almonds, cranberries, agave, vanilla and cayenne pepper; mix until the almonds are well coated.
3. Bake for 25-30 minutes. Turning them once.
4. Coat with sea salt and sesame seeds.

Prep time: 5 minutes
Bake time: 30 minutes

Nutrients per serving: Calories: 308, Total Fat: 19 g, Sat. Fat: 1g, Carbs: 33 g, Fiber: 6 g, Sugars: 21 g, Protein: 8 g, Sodium: 118 mg, Cholesterol: 0 mg

"The garden suggests there might be a place where we can meet nature halfway." Michael Pollan

Hearty Nachos

Nachos are a family favorite. The beauty of nachos is that they are mostly vegetarian, so a few substitutes and your family won't even notice the lack of meat. Nachos are a great way to combine high fiber foods like grains, beans and veggies in delicious way. The combination creates a blood sugar stabilizing snack that is filling and healthy. This recipe covers all of my targeted categories--anti-aging, reducing blood sugars, heart disease and obesity. Makes 8 servings.

2 cups of corn nacho chips

1 teaspoon of extra virgin olive oil

1/2 cup of yellow onions, chopped

2-3 garlic cloves, crushed

1 1/2 cups of pinto beans, cooked (15 ounce can, drained)

1/2 - 1 cup of organic vegetable broth

1/2 cup of scallions

2 cups of lettuce, shredded

1/2 cup of salsa or tomatoes

1/2 cup of guacamole

1/2 cup of black olives, chopped

1/4 cup of nutritional yeast

Ingredients:
1. In a large serving dish, add corn nachos.
2. In a sauté pan, add oil, onion and garlic; cook for 2 minutes.
3. Add pinto beans and 1/2 cup of broth; cook on medium heat for 4-5 minutes, until beans are warmed.
4. Use a potato masher to mash the beans into rough paste. Alternatively, turn off heat and in a blender add the beans and broth.
5. Puree for 45 seconds.
6. Pour the pureed beans over the nachos.
7. Add scallions, lettuce, salsa, guacamole, and black olives.
8. Sprinkle nutritional yeast over the top.

Prep time: 5 minutes
Cook time: 7 minutes

Nutrients per serving: Calories: 178, Total Fat: 5 g, Sat. Fat: 1g, Carbs: 27 g, Fiber: 6 g, Sugars: 1 g, Protein: 7 g, Sodium: 321 mg, Cholesterol: 0 mg

Artichoke Avocado Dip

Everyone loves chips and dip. Here is a simple dip that allows you to enjoy the crunch of chips and get a few servings of vegetables in too. Artichokes are antioxidant rich, so they're considered an anti-aging and anti-cancer food.
Makes 4 servings.

1 small avocado, chopped
1/4 cup of marinated
  artichokes
1 teaspoon of extra virgin
  olive oil
1/2 teaspoon of lemon juice

1/4 teaspoon of dried thyme
A pinch of sea salt
1/4 teaspoon of cumin
1 drop of maple syrup
1/4 teaspoon of garlic powder

1. Place all the ingredients in a food processor and pulse 15-30 seconds until chunky.
2. Serve with whole grain chips.

Prep time: 5 minutes
Cook time: 7 minutes

Nutrients per serving: Calories: 101, Total Fat: 9 g, Sat. Fat: 1g, Carbs: 7 g, Fiber: 4 g, Sugars: 1 g, Protein: 2 g, Sodium: 131 mg, Cholesterol: 0 mg

Tomatoes Bruschetta

There is nothing better than fresh organic tomatoes especially in late summer. Consider growing your own in a container on your porch or balcony. Tomatoes have antioxidants like lycopene and vitamin C that are essential for cell repair. Olive oil is a monounsaturated fatty acid (MUFAs) which is considered a healthy dietary fat important for heart and skin health. Makes 6 servings.

4 teaspoons of cashews

2 cups of tomatoes, diced

4 scallions, chopped

3 teaspoons of fresh parsley, chopped thin

2 teaspoons of olive oil

1/2 teaspoon of sea salt

1/2 teaspoon of fresh black pepper

Whole wheat baguette or flat bread cut into slices

Olive oil to brush bread

1. Take cashews and put in the food processor for 30 seconds. This makes cashew powder. Set aside.
2. In a bowl, add tomatoes, scallions, parsley, oil, salt, and pepper. Mix.
3. Place the slices of bread on a baking sheet.
4. Brush with olive oil.
5. Place the tomato mixture over the bread.
6. Place in the broiler for 1 minute.
7. Sprinkle cashew powder.
8. Serve while warm.

Prep time: 5 minutes
Cook time: 7 minutes

Nutrients per serving: Calories: 68, Total Fat: 4 g, Sat. Fat: 1g, Carbs: 7 g, Fiber: 2 g, Sugars: 3g, Protein: 2 g, Sodium: 125 mg, Cholesterol: 0 mg

Olive Tapenade

Olives are an anti-inflammatory perfect food!
They have also been shown to help with allergic responses by
reducing the histamine response. Having this snack is a great
way to get in healthy fats and soluble fiber. It balances blood
sugars while improving heart health and reducing cancer risk
all at the same time. Makes 6 servings.

1/2 cup of Kalamata olives pitted and loosely chopped

1/2 cup of green olives, pitted and loosely chopped

1/4 cup of red peppers

1 tablespoon of capers

2 garlic cloves

2 tablespoons of olive oil

1 tablespoon of fresh parsley, coarsely chopped

Juice of 1 lemon, freshly squeezed

1/4 teaspoon of fresh ground black pepper to taste

1. In a food processor, mix all the ingredients for 15 - 30 seconds until a course consistency is achieved.
2. Serve with whole wheat crackers or raw vegetables.

Prep time: 5 minutes

Nutrients per serving: Calories: 63, Total Fat: 6 g, Sat. Fat: 1g, Carbs: 4 g, Fiber: 1 g, Sugars: 0 g, Protein: 1 g, Sodium: 300 mg, Cholesterol: 0 mg

Sweet Plantains

Plantains are one of my favorite treats! They are sweet and crunchy! Plantains are high in vitamin A, potassium, magnesium and vitamin B6. They are high in fiber too. Pair with black beans for balanced snack! Plantains are nice as a side or dessert. Makes 6 servings.

3 large plantains   1/2 teaspoon of sea salt
2 teaspoons of coconut oil

1. Cut each plantain into diagonally slices, about a 1/4 inch thick.
2. Add coconut oil to a saucepan over medium heat.
3. Sauté plantain slices in a single layer for 3 minutes on each side until golden brown.
4. Serve immediately.

Prep time: 5 minutes
Cook time: 6-7 minutes

Nutrients per serving: Calories: 173, Total Fat: 2 g, Sat. Fat: 1 g, Carbs: 43 g, Fiber: 3 g, Sugars: 20 g, Protein: 2 g, Sodium: 122 mg, Cholesterol: 0 mg

"All the pre-made sauces in a jar, and frozen and canned vegetables, processed meats, and cheeses which are loaded with artificial ingredients and sodium can get in the way of a healthy diet. My number one advice is to eat fresh, and seasonally."
Todd English

Quick Tabbouleh

Chickpeas taste great and they're also very satisfying. In fact, chickpeas have been shown to support weight loss by reducing appetite. The fresh herbs and the zip of lemon makes it the perfect snack for a summer afternoon. You can serve this easy tabbouleh on lettuce, by itself, or in a pita pocket. Makes 6 servings.

1 cup of cooked couscous*

1 cup of cooked chickpeas (15 ounce can, drained)

1/4 cup of fresh parsley, chopped

1 tablespoon of fresh mint, chopped

1/4 cup of red onion, chopped

1/4 cup of roasted red pepper, chopped

1/2 cup of tomatoes, chopped

1/2 lemon, freshly squeezed

A pinch of sea salt

A pinch of black pepper

1. In a large bowl, add couscous, chickpeas, parsley, mint, onion, roasted red pepper and tomato; mix lightly.
2. Add lemon juice, salt and black pepper to taste. Mix well.
*To make this recipe gluten-free, replace couscous with quinoa.

Prep time: 8 minutes
Chill until ready to serve.

Nutrients per serving: Calories: 88, Total Fat: 1 g, Sat. Fat: 0g, Carbs: 18 g, Fiber: 3 g, Sugars: 1 g, Protein: 3 g, Sodium: 125 mg, Cholesterol: 0 mg

Daelicious Desserts

Chocolate Truffles

Chocolate is one of my favorite pleasures. Dark chocolate is high in antioxidants which are essential for healthy cells and cell repair in the anti-aging process. The truffles are sweet and satisfying because they are filled with fiber from the oats. This sweet treat also balances blood sugar while lowering cholesterol at the same time. Just remember, don't eat too many even though you will want to! Makes 24 truffles.

3/4 cup of oats

2 ounces of dark chocolate (at least 60% cacao), finely chopped

1 cup of pitted medjool dates, chopped

1 1/2 teaspoon of orange zest

A pinch of sea salt

*1/2 cup of shredded coconut

* optional

1. Place the oats in the food processor and blend into a fine powder - about 1 minute
2. Melt chocolate over a double boiler.
3. In the food processor bowl, add dates, orange zest, salt, and chocolate; mix for 1 minute.
4. Transfer to a glass bowl and chill for 2 hours
5. On a plate scatter the shredded coconut topping.
6. Scoop out 1 tablespoon of the dough into your hand and form a small ball
7. *Roll the small ball on the plate to cover with coconut topping.

Prep time: 10 minutes
Chill time: 1 hour

Nutrients per serving: Calories: 374, Total Fat: 9 g, Sat. Fat: 4 g, Carbs: 72 g, Fiber: 9 g, Sugars: 36 g, Protein: 8 g, Sodium: 120 mg, Cholesterol: 0 mg

Cranberry Granita

*This is a refreshing dessert or palate cleanser for the fall.
Cranberries have antioxidant, anti-inflammatory, and anti-
cancer properties which are all needed for optimal health.
Vitamin C is another key nutrient in this recipe because
it is found in several of the ingredients. The antioxidant
phytonutrients, including vitamin C are essential for the
restoration and repair of cells. This recipe is an anti-aging treat
for the cells and skin. Makes 6 servings.*

3 teaspoons of orange zest

1 1/2 seedless orange, slices

2 cups of cranberries

3 sweet soft pears, sliced

1/4 cup of agave nectar

1/4 cup of fresh squeezed
lime juice (2-3 limes)

Sprig of mint for garnish.

1. In a food processor combine orange zest, orange slices, cranberries, pears, agave nectar, and lime juice.
2. Puree for 2 minutes.
3. Taste and add agave nectar or lime juice as needed.
4. Pour the ingredients into the ice cream maker until soft and serve.

Prep time: 5 minutes
Chill time: 1-2 hours

Nutrients per serving: Calories: 159, Total Fat: 0 g, Sat. Fat: 0 g, Carbs: 42 g, Fiber: 8 g, Sugars: 23 g, Protein: 1 g, Sodium: 3 mg, Cholesterol: 0 mg

*"No one who cooks, cooks alone. Even at her most solitary,
a cook in the kitchen is surrounded by generations of cooks
past, the advice and menus of cooks present, the wisdom of
cookbook writers."*
Laurie Colwin

Old-Fashioned Apple Pie

If you love sweets like I do, consider this fruit based dessert because it is loaded with fiber and natural sweetness. Apples are getting attention for their polyphenol properties that help with cardiovascular disease. So it looks like an apple a day can keep the doctor away.
**Note: Trans-fatty acids are hidden in many baked goods, so make sure to use non-hydrogenated pie crusts.
Trans-fatty acids raise your bad cholesterol and lower your good cholesterol. They also raise your risk of developing type II diabetes. Makes 8 servings.

5 Granny Smith apples, cored, peeled and sliced

Zest of 1 lemon

2 tablespoons of lemon juice

1/2 cup of turbinado sugar

2 tablespoons of unbleached flour

1 teaspoons of ground cinnamon

1/2 teaspoon of grated nutmeg

1/2 teaspoon of ground cloves

1 pre-made, non-hydrogenated pie crust

1. Preheat oven to 400°F.
2. In a large bowl, combine apples, lemon zest, sugar, flour, cinnamon, nutmeg, and cloves.
3. Fill the pie crust with the apple mixture.
4. Lower the oven temperature to 375°F, place the pie in the oven and bake for 45 minutes.

Prep time: 10 minutes
Cook time: 45 minutes

Nutrients per serving: Calories: 229, Total Fat: 8 g, Sat. Fat: 2 g, Carbs: 40 g, Fiber: 4 g, Sugars: 25 g, Protein: 2 g, Sodium: 119 mg, Cholesterol: 0 mg

Coconut Vegan Ice Cream

Just because you are dairy-free doesn't mean you have to give up ice cream. The cashews and the coconut milk have a luscious and creamy texture because of the healthy fat. Cashews are packed with protein and fiber so they reduce heart disease and improve digestion. Coconut milk has medium-chain fatty acids that may increase metabolism and aid in weight loss. Makes 4 servings.

4 ounce can of coconut milk, frozen

1/4 cup of cashews

1/2 teaspoon of vanilla

1 teaspoon of agave nectar

1. Combine coconut milk, cashews, vanilla and agave in the Vitamix on high.
2. Using the tamper, mash the ingredients against the blades to create the soft serve consistency.
3. Start with the lowest speed and increase to 10 on low then move to high speed. Continue for 2-3 minutes until nuts and coconut milk are blended.

Prep time: 5 minutes
Chill time: keep chilled until ready to serve

Nutrients per serving: Calories: 137, Total Fat: 12 g, Sat. Fat: 6 g, Carbs: 6 g, Fiber: 1 g, Sugars: 2 g, Protein: 3 g, Sodium: 5 mg, Cholesterol: 0 mg

Silky Strawberry Ice Cream

The Vitamix or a high-speed blender is the best way to get a smooth soft-serve consistency. The healthy oils found in the almonds and pecans create a creamy soft serve texture when combined with fruit. The gift of this dessert is that it is filled with good fats, proteins and fiber that help to balance blood sugars while giving you a sweet treat. Makes 4 servings.

1/4 cup of almonds

1/4 cup of pecans

2 cups of organic frozen
strawberries

2 tablespoons of agave nectar

1. In a Vitamix or high speed blender, add the almonds, pecans, strawberries, and agave.

2. Using the tamper, mash the ingredients against the blades to create the soft serve consistency.

3. Start with the lowest speed and increase to 10 on low, then move to high speed. Continue for 2-3 minutes until nuts are completely blended with the fruit.

Prep time 5 minutes
Chill time: keep chilled until ready to serve

Nutrients per serving: Calories: 167, Total Fat: 14 g, Sat. Fat: 1g, Carbs: 11 g, Fiber: 4 g, Sugars: 6 g, Protein: 4 g, Sodium: 1 mg, Cholesterol: 0 mg

Berry Pear Pie

This is a great fall pie that's sweet and tart at the same time. Both cranberries and pears are high in antioxidant and anti-inflammatory properties to reduce chronic inflammation. These properties are important for anti-aging and to promote heart health. This pie is a safe treat for diabetics as the fiber supports stable blood sugar levels. Makes 8 servings.
*Note: Trans-fatty acids are hidden in many baked goods so make sure to use non-hydrogenated pie crusts. Trans-fatty acids raise your bad cholesterol and lower your good cholesterol. They also raise your risk of developing type II diabetes.

3 medium Anjou or Bartlett pears, seeded, peeled and sliced

1/2 cup of fresh cranberries

1 cup of turbinado sugar

1 heaping tablespoon of flour

1 teaspoon of ground cinnamon

1/4 teaspoon of ground ginger

1/4 teaspoon of sea salt

1/2 cup of orange juice

2 teaspoons of grated orange zest

1 pre-made non-hydrogenated pie crust

1. Preheat oven to 425°F.
2. In a large bowl, add pears, cranberries, sugar, flour, cinnamon, ginger, salt, orange juice and orange zest. Mix and pour into the pie crust.
3. Bake for 15 minutes, and then lower the heat to 350°F; bake for 30 minutes until pie is golden brown.

Prep time: 8 minutes
Cook time: 45 minutes

Nutrients per serving: Calories: 149, Total Fat: 0 g, Sat. Fat: 0g, Carbs: 39 g, Fiber: 3 g, Sugars: 33 g, Protein: 0 g, Sodium: 60 mg, Cholesterol: 0 mg

Apple Crisp

What do I love about apple crisps? The oat-based granola crust adds fiber and protein to your dessert. One of the health benefits of oatmeal is found in its soluble fiber. Soluble fiber binds to cholesterol and cholesterol based hormones and pulls them into the digestive tract so they can be eliminated from the body. Apples are also a good source of dietary fiber, but the phytonutrients in apples can also help regulate blood sugar levels. The combination of the two makes a great dessert.
Makes 8 servings.
You can use berries, pears, peaches or plums in this basic crisp recipe depending on what's fresh and in season.

6 Granny Smith apples, washed, peeled and sliced

1 tablespoon of fresh lemon juice

2 teaspoons of ground cinnamon

1 teaspoon of ground cardamom

1/3 cup frozen apple juice concentrate, thawed

1 teaspoon safflower oil

1 1/2 cup of your favorite granola

1. Preheat oven to 350°F.
2. In a large bowl, add sliced apples, lemon juice, cinnamon, cardamom and apple juice.
3. Mix gently so you don't crush the apples.
4. Lightly grease a casserole dish or pie pan; pour apples into the dish.
5. Bake for 30 minutes.
6. Remove from the oven. Sprinkle the granola over the apples and bake for another 15 minutes until the apples are bubbling.
7. Remove and let cool for 10 minutes.

Prep time: 12 minutes
Bake time: 45 minutes

Nutrients per serving: Calories: 196, Total Fat: 6 g, Sat. Fat: 1g, Carbs: 33 g, Fiber: 6 g, Sugars: 20 g, Protein: 4 g, Sodium: 8 mg, Cholesterol: 0 mg

Kabocha Squash Pie

At the farmers' market and I saw a beautiful orange squash, so I bought it to make pie. Winter squash like kabocha has rich sources of omega 3 essential fatty acids and beta-carotene. These anti-inflammatory nutrients are essential for restoring health from illnesses like heart health, pre-diabetes, diabetes, and they reverse the aging process. Makes 8 servings.

1 kabocha squash	1 teaspoon of vanilla extract
1 1/2 cup of raw pecans	1 teaspoon of ground allspice
1/2 cup of turbinado sugar	1/4 cup of maple syrup
1/3 cup of coconut milk or lite coconut milk, depending on preference	1 egg substitute or (1 tablespoon ground flaxseed and 3 tablespoon warm water)

Three Simple Ways to Get the Meat Out of a Pumpkin/Squash for your favorite recipes:

On the stove: Place the pumpkin/squash in a pan of water on medium heat. Cook for 30-60 minutes or until the skin can be pierced easily with a knife.

In the oven: Put several holes in the skin of the pumpkin/squash. Heat oven to 400° F and bake for 50-60 minutes or until the skin can be pierced easily with a knife.

In the microwave: Place the pumpkin/squash in a microwave safe dish. Pierce with a knife to make several holes in the skin. Heat on high for 7- 10 minutes or until the skin can be pierced by a knife easily.

Once the pumpkin has been softened, scoop out the seeds and discard or save them to roast in the oven. Scoop out the meat of the pumpkin and use for a variety of dishes, like the Pumpkin Bread or Acorn Squash with Fruit Filling.

(continued on next page)

1. Pierce holes in the kabocha squash and place on a baking sheet for about 50 minutes in the oven at 375° F. Take out of the oven and let cool.
2. Reduce oven temperature to 350°F. Once cool, peel off the outside of the squash. Cut in half and scoop out the seeds.
3. Scoop out the inner flesh and set aside. Consider freezing unused portion for next time.
4. To make the crust: In a blender or food processor break pecans into a course meal.
5. Add turbinado sugar and pulse 5-10 times.
6. Remove from appliance and use mixture to cover the bottom of the pie plate.
7. Cook in the oven for 10 minutes at 300° F.
8. In the food processor, add 3 cups of kabocha squash, coconut milk, vanilla, ground allspice, maple syrup and egg substitute. Blend for 45 seconds.
9. Pour into the crust and bake for 50 minutes or until firm.

Prep time: 5 minutes
Bake time: 50 minutes squash/60 minutes for the pie

Nutrients per serving: Calories: 252, Total Fat: 17 g, Sat. Fat: 3g, Carbs: 26 g, Fiber: 2 g, Sugars: 20 g, Protein: 3 g, Sodium: 3 mg, Cholesterol: 0 mg

"If more of us valued food and cheer and song above hoarded gold, it would be a merrier world."
J.R.R. Tolkien

Sweet Potato Pie

Sweet potatoes are so versatile and healthy but my favorite way to eat them hands down is in a pie! Sweet potatoes are root vegetables but they are prized for their ability to balance blood sugars by modulating insulin metabolism. This makes them perfect for regulating diabetes and weight loss.
Makes 8 servings.

4-6 small-medium sweet potatoes, rinsed

1 egg substitute, or (1 tablespoon of ground flaxseed and 3 tablespoons of water)

1/4 cup of turbinado sugar

1 teaspoon of cinnamon

1 teaspoon of nutmeg

1/4 teaspoon of allspice

1/4 teaspoon of sea salt

1/4 cup of milk substitute (rice milk adds sweetness)

Pie crust

1 1/2 cup of raw pecans

1/2 cup of turbinado sugar

1. Preheat the oven to 400°F.
2. With a sharp knife, pierce the sweet potatoes several times. Bake on a cookie sheet for 45 minutes or until soft.
3. Let the sweet potatoes cool to the touch; then peel the skin off. The skin should easily fall off the meat of the potato.
4. Turn the oven down to 375°F.
5. Place skinned potatoes in a bowl or food processor; add egg substitute, sugar, cinnamon, nutmeg, allspice, salt and milk substitute. Mix for 2 minutes.
5. To make the crust: In a blender or food processor, break pecans into a course meal.
6. Add turbinado sugar and pulse 5-10 times.
7. Remove from appliance; use mixture to cover the bottom of pie plate.
8. Pour into a pie crust; bake for 50-60 minutes or until firm.

Prep time: 5 minutes
Bake time: 45 minutes squash/55 minutes for the pie

Nutrients per serving: Calories: 267, Total Fat: 15 g, Sat. Fat: 1g, Carbs: 33 g, Fiber: 5 g, Sugars: 17 g, Protein: 3 g, Sodium: 106 mg, Cholesterol: 0 mg

Poached Pears

This is an easy recipe that looks fancy, but it is extremely easy to make. Pears have phytonutrients called flavonoids that have been shown to reduce the risk of type II diabetes. Some of these flavonoids are also antioxidant and anti-inflammatory, so they reduce cancer risk as well. Pears are a great fall fruit to have as a snack as well. Makes 6 servings.

3 pears, halved, seeded and peeled

4 cups of water

1 lemon, squeezed

1 teaspoon of vanilla extract

1 teaspoon of cinnamon

2 teaspoons of maple syrup

1. In a 4-quart pan add water and bring to a boil.
2. Add pears and cook for 8-10 minutes or until tender. Remove to cool.
3. Pierce pears in several places for syrup.
4. In a small bowl, mix lemon juice, vanilla, cinnamon and maple syrup.
5. Pour over pears.

Prep time: 8 minutes
Bake time: 10 minutes

Nutrients per serving: Calories: 36, Total Fat: 0 g, Sat. Fat: 0g, Carbs: 9 g, Fiber: 2 g, Sugars: 6 g, Protein: 0 g, Sodium: 2 mg, Cholesterol: 0 mg

Chocolate Pudding

This simple pudding recipe is one that any chocolate lover will flip for. The secret ingredient is avocado. Avocadoes have the kind of healthy fat we need to create essential hormones. The combination of healthy fats and carbohydrates in avocado supports blood sugar regulation. Avocadoes have anti-inflammatory properties important for heart health and reduction of inflammation from diabetes. It helps to create satiation for weight loss too. Makes 6 servings.

2 ripe avocadoes

1/2 cup of raspberries

6 tablespoons of dark unsweetened cocoa powder

1/4 cup of grade B maple syrup

Pinch of salt

1 teaspoon of vanilla

1/2 teaspoon of balsamic vinegar

1/2 teaspoon of fresh lime juice

1. Place all ingredients into a blender or food processor for 1 minute or until well blended.
2. Chill for 15 minutes.
3. Serve immediately.

Prep time: 5 minutes
Bake time: 10 minutes

Nutrients per serving: Calories: 163, Total Fat: 11 g, Sat. Fat: 2g, Carbs: 20 g, Fiber: 7 g, Sugars: 9 g, Protein: 3 g, Sodium: 15 mg, Cholesterol: 0 mg

'The easiest diet is, you know, eat vegetables, eat fresh food. Just a really sensible healthy diet like you read about all the time."
Drew Carey

Blueberry Cobbler

Surprisingly blueberries have been shown to have a favorable impact on diabetes, insulin resistance and metabolic syndrome. Blueberries contain soluble, insoluble fiber and tannins that support digestive health. They've been shown to help ease the complications of peptic ulcers, constipation and diarrhea. Blueberries have one the highest capacities to destroy free radicals, so they help the whole body. Blueberries also help relieve oxidative stress in the brain due to aging. Blueberries have been studied for their anti-cancer properties. They support cardiovascular health by helping to maintain the integrity of blood, which prevents varicose veins and hemorrhoids. When choosing granola, read the labels to make sure there is not too much sugar. I recommend the Bear Naked brand. Makes 8 servings.

6 cups of blueberries, fresh or frozen

3/4 cups of raw sugar

Juice of 1 lemon

2 teaspoons of corn starch

2 teaspoons of warm water

1 1/2 cups of granola

1. In a 6-quart saucepan, add blueberries to a medium low heat.
2. Add sugar and lemon juice to the blueberries.
3. In a small bowl, add cornstarch and warm water; whisk until well mixed.
4. Cook for 8 minutes; until the blueberries are soft and popped.
5. Transfer blueberry mixture to a baking dish; cover with granola.
6. Bake for 20 minutes at 375°F. Granola will be golden brown.
7. Let Cool for 20 minutes before serving.

Prep time: 5 minutes
Cook time: 8 minutes
Bake time: 20 minutes
Cool time: 20 minutes

Nutrients per serving: Calories: 256, Total Fat: 6 g, Sat. Fat: 1g, Carbs: 49 g, Fiber: 5 g, Sugars: 35 g, Protein: 4 g, Sodium: 7 mg, Cholesterol: 0 mg

Fruit Parfait

This is a no cook recipe that can be used as a dessert or breakfast. It is high in antioxidants because of the strawberries, blueberries and mangos. The high antioxidants in berries have been proven to improve heart health, prevent aging, and to have a positive effect on balancing blood sugars. Makes 6 servings.

4 cup of non-dairy yogurt (coconut yogurt, soy yogurt, etc.)

1/2 teaspoon of vanilla extract

1/2 teaspoon of maple syrup

1 cup of strawberries, chopped

1 cup of blueberries, whole

1 cup of mangos, chopped

1/4 cup of sliced almond

1. In a small bowl, mix non-dairy yogurt, vanilla extract and maple syrup.
2. In a parfait cup or martini glass, layer mango pieces (about 1/2 cup of fruit).
3. Next layer the yogurt mixture about (1/4 cup of yogurt),
4. Next layer blueberries (about 1/2 cup of fruit).
5. Next layer yogurt mixture (1/4 cup of yogurt).
6. Next layer strawberries (about 1/2 cup of fruit).
7. Finally sprinkle the almond on top.
8. Chill for 15 minutes.
9. Serve immediately.

Prep time: 10 minutes

Nutrients per serving: Calories: 169, Total Fat: 4 g, Sat. Fat: 3g, Carbs: 29 g, Fiber: 3 g, Sugars: 21 g, Protein: 5 g, Sodium: 15 mg, Cholesterol: 0 mg

Chia Berry Pudding

*Chia seeds have gained popularity because they are
an important source of omega-3 fatty acids.
Omega-3 essential fatty acids reduce inflammation and
increase the restoration of cells. Coconut milk is a source of
healthy fat that supports digestion. Makes 6 servings.*

1/4 cup of chia seeds

3/4 cup of coconut milk

1/2 cup of water

1 teaspoon of pure vanilla
extract

1/4 teaspoon of sea salt

3/4 teaspoon of maple syrup

1 cup of mixed berries
(blueberries and
strawberries)

1. Mix chia seeds, coconut milk, water, vanilla, salt, and maple syrup in a bowl; refrigerate for 2 hours.

2. Layer the chia pudding; add a layer of berries; continue until you have created 2 layers of each.

***Note: You can also use 1/2 teaspoon of agave nectar if you are concerned about blood sugar levels.

Prep time: 10 minutes
Chill time: 2 hours

Nutrients per serving: Calories: 180, Total Fat: 13 g, Sat. Fat: 8g, Carbs: 14 g, Fiber: 6 g, Sugars: 5 g, Protein: 3 g, Sodium: 126 mg, Cholesterol: 0 mg

Flourless Peanut Butter Dark Chocolate Chunk Cookies

These cookies are packed with protein, so they are a blood sugar balancing sweet treat. Peanut butter is rich in monounsaturated fats. This is a good fat that is important for heart heath, blood sugar balancing and stress. Peanuts provide resveratrol, the phytonutrient found in red wine that reverses aging. Both peanut butter and dark chocolate are high in antioxidants. Since these cookies are flourless they are packed with protein without the extra simple carbohydrates. Makes 12 cookies.

1 tablespoon of ground flax seed

3 tablespoons of warm water

1 cup of unsalted chunky peanut butter

3/4 cup of Sucanat

1/2 teaspoon of baking soda

1/4 teaspoon of sea salt

3 ounces of 70% dark chocolate broken into small pieces

1. In medium bowl, add the ground flax seed and water. Mix and let sit for 5 minutes.
2. Preheat oven to 350°F.
3. To the bowl, add peanut butter, Sucanat, baking soda, and salt; stir until well mixed.
4. Stir in chocolate.
5. Use a tablespoon to scoop dough onto parchment-lined baking sheets.
6. Bake for 8-10 minutes or until lightly browned.
7. Let cool on baking sheets for 5 minutes before serving.

Prep time: 5 minutes
Bake time: 10 minutes
Cool time: 10 minutes

Nutrients per serving: Calories: 165, Total Fat: 07 g, Sat. Fat: 3g, Carbs: 15 g, Fiber: 2 g, Sugars: 12 g, Protein: 4 g, Sodium: 72 mg, Cholesterol: 0 mg

Bibliography

Ambrosone CB, Tang L. Cruciferous vegetable intake and cancer prevention: role of nutrigenetics. Cancer Prev Res (Phila Pa). 2009 Apr;2(4):298-300. 2009.

Awad AB, Chan KC, Downie AC, Fink CS. Peanuts as a source of beta-sitosterol, a sterol with anticancer properties. Nutr Cancer 2000;36(2): 238-241. 2000. PMID:10890036.

Basu A, Rhone M and Lyons TJ. Berries: emerging impact on cardiovascular health. Nutr Rev. 2010 Mar;68(3):168-77. Review. 2010.

Blomhoff R, Carlsen MH, Andersen LF, Jacobs DR Jr. Health benefits of nuts: potential role of antioxidants. Br J Nutr. 2006 Nov;96 Suppl 2:S52-60. 2006. PMID:17125534.

DeFuria J, Bennett G, Strissel KJ et al. Dietary . Dietary Blueberry Attenuates Whole-Body Insulin Resistance in High Fat-Fed Mice by Reducing Adipocyte Death and Its Inflammatory Sequelae. J Nutr. 2009 August; 139(8): 1510-1516. doi: 10.3945/jn.109.105155. 2009.

Elson M. Haas, MD, The Detox Diet: A How-To & When-To Guide for Cleansing the Body. Berkeley, Celestial Arts, 2004.

Elson M. Haas, MD, Staying Healthy with the Seasons. Berkeley, Celestial Arts, 2003.

Higdon JV, Delage B, Williams DE, et al. Cruciferous Vegetables and Human Cancer Risk: Epidemiologic Evidence and Mechanistic Basis. Pharmacol Res. 2007 March; 55(3): 224-236. 2007.

Josse AR, Kendall CW, Augustin LS, Ellis PR, Jenkins DJ. Almonds and postprandial glycemia--a dose-response study. Metabolism. 2007 Mar;56(3):400-4. 2007. PMID:17292730.

Li F, Hullar MAJ, Schwarz Y, et al. Human Gut Bacterial Communities Are Altered by Addition of Cruciferous Vegetables to a Controlled Fruit- and Vegetable-Free Diet. Journal of Nutrition, Vol. 139, No. 9, 1685-1691, September 2009. 2009.

Murty CM, Pittaway JK and Ball MJ. Chickpea supplementation in an Australian diet affects food choice, satiety and bowel health. Appetite. 2010 Apr;54(2):282-8. Epub 2009 Nov 27. 2010.

A

Mateljan, G. (2006). The world's healthiest foods: essential guide for the healthiest way of eating. Seattle, Wash.: George Mateljan Foundation.

Merck Manual, Merck Research Laboratories, Whitehouse Station, N.J. Copyright © 2006-2007.

Pittaway JK, Ahuja KDK, Cehun M et al. Dietary Supplementation with Chickpeas for at Least 5 Weeks Results in Small but Significant Reductions in Serum Total and Low-Density Lipoprotein Cholesterols in Adult Women and Men. Annals of Nutrition & Metabolism. Basel: Feb 2007. Vol. 50, Iss. 6; p. 512-518. 2007.

Pittaway JK, Ahuja KDK, Robertson IK et al. Effects of a Controlled Diet Supplemented with Chickpeas on Serum Lipids, Glucose Tolerance, Satiety and Bowel Function. J. Am. Coll. Nutr., Aug 2007; 26: 334 - 340.. 2007.

Pittaway JK, Robertson IK and Ball MJ. Chickpeas may influence fatty acid and fiber intake in an ad libitum diet, leading to small improvements in serum lipid profile and glycemic control. J Am Diet Assoc. 2008 Jun;108(6):1009-13. 2008.

R. A. I. Ekanayaka, N. K. Ekanayaka, B. Perera, and P. G. S. M. De Silva, "Impact of a Traditional Dietary Supplement with Coconut Milk and Soya Milk on the Lipid Profile in Normal Free Living Subjects," Journal of Nutrition and Metabolism, vol. 2013, Article ID 481068, 11 pages, 2013. doi:10.1155/2013/481068.

Russell B. Marz , Nutrition from Marz,. Quiet Lion Press, 2nd edition, 1999.

Scalbert, A., Johnson, I. T., & Saltmarsh, M. (2005). Polyphenols: antioxidants and beyond1,2,3. The American Journal of Clinical Nutrition, 81(1), 215S-217S.

B

About the Author

Dr. Daemon Jones, "Dr. Dae," graduated from Northwestern University with a degree in Economics in 1992. After working as a successful consultant for 6 years in corporate America, she found her purpose and her passion--naturopathic medicine. She entered naturopathic medical school and graduated as one of the top 10 in her class at the University of Bridgeport's College of Naturopathic Medicine. She returned to her hometown of Washington, DC to build her private practice and to support the community in creating healthy lives.

In the last 11 years, Dr. Dae has become a local, national, and international expert on lifestyle medicine and the prevention of chronic diseases. She focuses on educating and empowering her patients on how to reverse and prevent chronic diseases. Her goal is to share with people how to create holistic health by using a combination of safe and effective conventional and natural methods.

Dr. Dae specializes in the reversal and prevention of diabetes, hormonal imbalances, metabolism issues, and weight loss challenges. In her private practice in the Washington DC area, she uses conventional medicine to diagnose and to monitor her patients, along with proven naturopathic therapies to treat them. She uses effective and successful protocols that include diet, nutrition, exercise, and stress management tools to improve the health of her patients.

Dr. Dae writes about how to use lifestyle medicine to improve people's overall health and wellness. She is a staff writer for EmpowHer.com. She has also been featured on YahooHealth.com and FoxNewsHealth.com.

As a speaker, Dr. Dae combines humor and layman's language to explain how our bodies work and the connection between our health and disease. She then shares practical tips about how people can improve their habits to transform themselves into healthier and more energetic beings.

She is also an authority on diet and nutrition. Dr. Dae creates simple recipes that simultaneously tantalize the taste buds and heal the body. She has many years of conducting cooking demonstrations and preparing tasty and nutritional food for audiences around the country from recipes designed to improve health. Her books, *Daelicious! Recipes for Vibrant Living and Eat More Plants!* were developed from her healthy cooking demonstrations. Her books emphasize how to use food as medicine to improve chronic illness.

C

D

INDEX

Great Beginnings

Almond Coconut Smoothie.. 9

Almond Milk 13

Apple Cucumber Ginger
Fresh Juice 14

Avocado Delight 9

Banana Bliss Pancakes 1

Blueberry Antioxidant
Blast Smoothie.............. 12

Carrot Apple Fresh Juice .. 14

Chia Seed Raspberry Jam ... 2

Chocolate Peanut Butter
Cup Smoothie 10

Cinnamon Almond Butter
Smoothie 19

Cool As A Cucumber
Fresh Juice 15

Cucumber Mint Lime
Fresh Juice 17

Kale Celery Cucumber
Apple Fresh Juice 17

Kale Orange Strawberry
Fresh Juice 16

Kale Pear Mint Fresh
Juice........................... 16

Oatmeal Smoothie 10

Old Fashioned Oatmeal 3

Peach Berry Pleasure
Smoothie 11

Pink Lady Fresh Juice 15

Pumpkin Bread.................. 8

Quick Quinoa Breakfast...... 4

Sautéed Apples 5

Spinach Lemonade 18

Strawberry Banana
Surprise Smoothie 11

Sweet Potato Hash
Browns 6

Tofu Scramble 7

Satisfying Soups

Basic Veggie Stock 21

Black Bean Chili 31

Comforting Carrot Soup 23

Curry Pumpkin Soup 26

Fantastically Fresh
Tomato Soup 24

Green Lentil Soup 27

Green Split Pea Soup 25

Pink Lentil Soup 29

Roasted Butternut Squash
Soup............................. 28

Spice It Up Gazpacho
Soup............................. 30

Velvety Beet Soup 32

Very Veggie Udon Soup 22

Spectacularly Simple Salads

Asian Cole Slaw 41

Basic Salad Dressing 33

Bulgur Wheat Salad.......... 43

Citrus Berry Salad
Dressing 34

Couscous Olive Salad 54

Cranberry Pecan Salad 45

Fruity Fall Field Salad....... 44

Garlicky Kale Salad........... 39

Lemon Citrus Dressing 33

Lime Mint Cilantro
Dressing 35

Mango Orange Salad......... 53

Minty Lentil Salad............. 52

Oh My Darling Clementine
Salad 49

On a Mission Fig Salad 47

Orange Rosemary Salad.... 42

Rice Noodle Salad with
    Lime Peanut Dressing.... 55

Strawberry Spinach
    Crunch 48

Stress-Busting Salad 37

Summer's Sensational
    Salad 46

Surprise! It's Kale in A
    Salad 50

Tangy Couscous Salad...... 36

Tomato-Basil Chickpea
    Salad 51

Two Tomato Salad 38

Wilted Salad with Quinoa.. 40

Exciting Entrees

Bella Burgers.................... 65

Bok Choy Stir-Fry............. 58

Curry Sweet Potatoes........ 66

Eggplant Envelopes........... 68

Eggplant Lasagna 67

Hummus Half-Moon Pies .. 69

Lentil Quinoa Salad 60

Lime Coconut Chickpeas .. 76

Mediterranean Stuffed
    Zucchini 59

Nut Loaf 70

Roasted Vegetable
    Flatbread 74

Spicy Cashew Green
    Beans 63

Sunchoke Stir-fry 64

Sweet and Sassy Chickpea
    Soubios......................... 77

Sweet Potato Stir-Fry 61

Taco Tuesday.................... 75

Vegetable Enchiladas........ 73

Vegetable Pasta with
    Pesto............................. 57

Vegetarian Lettuce
    Wraps 71

Veggie Ciabatta
    Sandwich....................... 72

Veggies coated with
    Pesto............................. 62

Whole Grains Goodness

Brown Rice with Beans 85

Butternut Squash
    Risotto 79

Butternut Squash with
    Quinoa.......................... 87

'Cause it's just that good
    Corn Salad..................... 84

Cornbread Dressing.......... 86

Lime Cilantro Brown
    Rice 89

Nutty Rice with
    Mushrooms.................... 83

Pasta Medley 88

Simply Barley 82

Wild Rice with Roasted
    Nuts 81

Vibrant Vegetables

Basically Fantastic
    Brussels Sprouts 97

Cranberry Relish............. 107

Cranberry Relish Plus..... 108

Curried Chard and
    Potatoes....................... 102

Curried Mixed Greens....... 99

Fruit-Filled Acorn
    Squash 98

Minty Summer Squash 94

Mushroom Gravy............ 106

Piquant Tomato Sauce.... 105

Roasted Beets 110

Roasted Butternut squash........................ 109

Roasted Vegetables 101

Sautéed Cabbage 95

Savory Sweet Potatoes 93

Spaghetti Squash Pasta .. 103

Steamed Broccoli with a Twist.............................. 96

Sweet Sautéed Kale........... 92

Sweet Swiss Chard 100

Tomato Basil Sauce 104

Vegetarian Collard Greens........................... 91

Coconut Vegan Ice Cream............................ 126

Cranberry Granita 124

Flourless Peanut Butter Dark Chocolate Chunk Cookies 138

Fruit Parfait.................... 136

Kabocha Squash Pie 130

Old-Fashioned Apple Pie 125

Poached Pears 133

Silky Strawberry Ice Cream............................ 127

Sweet Potato Pie 132

Supercharged Snacks

Artichoke Avocado Dip.... 118

Black Bean Salsa............. 112

Glazed Almonds.............. 116

Hearty Nachos 117

Olive Tapenade 120

Pineapple Salsa 111

Quick Tabbouleh 122

Roasted pumpkin seeds.. 115

Roasted Red Pepper Hummus 113

Super Simple Guacamole.................... 114

Sweet Plantains 121

Tomatoes Bruschetta...... 119

Traditional Salsa Recipe.. 111

Daelicious Desserts

Apple Crisp...................... 129

Berry Pear Pie................. 128

Blueberry Cobbler........... 135

Chia Berry Pudding 137

Chocolate Pudding.......... 134

Chocolate Truffles........... 123